Monetary Policy and the Federal Funds Market

for Stanley and Roy Boughton

Monetary Policy and the Federal Funds Market

James M. Boughton

Duke University Press Durham, N. C. 1972

© 1970, 1972, Duke University Press

L.C.C. card no. 74-172018

I.S.B.N. 0-8223-0287-x

Printed in the United States of America

Preface

This book has evolved over a period of six years, inspired by a concern for studying the nature of the influences exerted on the United States economy by commercial banks in their capacity as private firms. I have attempted over that time to distill that general concern into a tractable topic, which is manifested here as a study of the influence of an interbank lending market on various demand-for-cash functions and hence on aggregate financial multipliers. The result can be viewed as a particular study of what I consider to be the general problem of understanding the relationship between commercial and central bankers in guiding the financial factors in our economy.

I have benefited from much counsel on this project. Numerous officials throughout the Federal Reserve System have answered even more numerous questions for me. Charles T. Taylor, Harry Brandt, and Paul A. Crowe of the Federal Reserve Bank of Atlanta piloted me through one of the early stages of my work; Leonall Andersen and his colleagues provided several beneficial suggestions at a seminar at the Federal Reserve Bank of St. Louis; and Frank deLeeuw, formerly on the staff of the Board of Governors, has assisted me in understanding the nature of financial models. Among the commercial bankers with whom I have discussed various aspects of this work, I would like especially to thank Stanley R. Boughton, James Posthauer, and Gordon Gaylord of Purdue National Bank of Lafayette, Indiana; G. Frank Holland, formerly of American Fletcher National Bank of Indianapolis; Edward Malloy of Irving Trust Company; G. Harlow Gardner of Manufacturers Hanover Trust Company; Lawrence Smith of United California Bank; and Al Smith of North Carolina National Bank.

Most of the work on the book was completed while I was a student at Duke University and the University of Michigan; a preliminary version was submitted as a doctoral dissertation in 1969.[1] My debt to Professors

---

1. James M. Boughton, "The Effect of an Active Market in Federal Funds on the Transmission of Monetary Policy," Ph.D. dissertation, Duke University, 1969.

Thomas H. Naylor and William P. Yohe is incalculable. I also received much
help from Professors David G. Davies and Peter B. Clark of Duke University,
David Brophy of Michigan, and Elmus Wicker of Indiana University; and from
fellow students Eduard H. Brau, W. Earl Sasser, and Ellen Temple. Miss
Ruth Henderson patiently prepared the typescript from which this book was
printed, and Mr. Mushtaq Ahmad assisted in preparing the index. Financial
support from the Federal Reserve Bank of Atlanta, The National Science
Foundation (Grants GS-1926 and GS-2981), the Social System Simulation Program of Duke University, and the American Bankers Association provided the
fuel for the several stages of the project. The Journal of Finance kindly
provided permission to use previously published material. The editorial
assistance from my wife Susan in preparing the manuscript will add much to
whatever pleasure the reader may derive from the following pages; however,
all of the individuals listed here will be relieved to see that I accept
the customary responsibility for any remaining errors.

                                        James M. Boughton
                                        August 1, 1971

Contents

List of Tables and Figures

Introduction

A commercial bank makes a loan to another commercial bank. An interest rate is agreed upon, and maturity of the loan is set at one business day. The transfer is to be completed this morning and will be reversed tomorrow. In this manner, several billion dollars change hands each day; collectively, these loans constitute the interbank market for Federal Reserve funds, commonly called the Federal funds market.[1]

Approximately three thousand banks participate in this market. Some banks enter as lenders, some as borrowers, and a great many of them engage in both borrowing and lending on different days or even on the same day. For some banks the market represents a continuous source of lendable funds. For others it is a convenient means of disposing of idle balances either irregularly or continuously. Still other banks use the market to adjust their reserve positions in either direction in order to satisfy legal reserve requirements each week without accumulating excess non-earning assets. The market therefore is an alternative to the Federal Reserve discount window, to transactions in secondary reserve assets, to changes in business or consumer lending, to the attraction of new deposits--particu-

---

1. Not all interbank loans are loans of Federal funds. As used throughout this work, a loan of Federal funds is defined as "any transaction involving the acquisition or disposal of immediately available funds for one business day only, at a specified rate of interest. ...Typically, Federal funds transactions involve the acquisition or disposal of title to reserve balances of member banks at Federal Reserve Banks; in contrast to a check drawn on a clearing house bank collectible the next day. However, Federal funds also include all transactions through credits or debits on new or existing correspondent balances, when such transactions otherwise meet the above definition of Federal funds. ...Not included are any purchases and sales under contracts which are specifically written to mature in two or more business days, or require advance notice to terminate. But all continuing contracts, which are defined as those which remain in effect for more than one day but have no specified maturity and do not require advance notice to terminate, are included." Harry Brandt and Paul A. Crowe, "Trading in Federal Funds by Banks in the Southeast," Southern Journal of Business, III (April, 1968), note 6. The present study is further restricted to loans between commercial banks.

larly negotiable time certificates--and to the myriad of other forms of borrowing or lending which comprise the daily operation of a commercial bank.

There exists today an organized but decentralized nationwide market in
Federal funds. In addition to the thousands of member banks which trade
such funds there are a number of non-bank participants, particularly brokers. Quite a few banks act as intermediaries in the market as a service to
their correspondents. Large regional clearing operations exist in Chicago,
Dallas, San Francisco, and most other reserve cities throughout the country.
The heart of the market, however, is in New York City. There the largest
and most regular borrowers and all of the major brokers are headquartered.
One of the most striking characteristics of the market for Federal funds is
that it usually serves to funnel bank reserves from all over the country
into a few large banks in New York City.

Each of these observations will be expanded at length in the chapters
to follow. Perhaps, though, this brief introduction will be sufficient to
illustrate the sort of economic and social issues that are raised by the
existence of the Federal funds market. The market came into being as a
means of adjusting to disequilibria in the distribution of bank reserves,
and it still performs that function today. Reserves are thereby redistri-
buted among banks and among regions, from the areas of lesser demand for
bank assets to areas of greater demand. When there is a general shortage
of reserves, the market's role as a source of funds may prove to be a mir-
age as bankers bid against themselves to acquire resources from one another. What appears in prosperity to be a source of liquidity could prove
in stress to be entirely illiquid.

These potential problems could affect the conduct and the transmission
of monetary policies. However, the question of how this interbank adjustment mechanism affects public policy is not easily answered. The primary
purpose of the present study is to attempt to provide such an answer.

The problem with which we shall be dealing can be made more explicit
by grouping its possible solutions into two categories, two schools of
thought. The first possibility is that the Federal funds market is an aid
to the formulation and implementation of monetary policy, that it lubri-
cates the transmission of policies from their source to their ultimate
targets. The authors of this point of view may be referred to as the
"lubricationists." In general this school of thought holds that the effects of using policy instruments such as open market operations and the

Federal Reserve discount rate are enhanced by the existence of the Federal funds market because of the way the market acts to transmit changes in bank reserve positions from the central money markets to the thousands of banks throughout the country.

The second possibility is that the funds market may offset, at least partially, the effects of monetary policy. The students of this point of view may be described as the "offset" school. Here changes in the supply of reserves or in the cost of credit, induced by the Federal Reserve, are thought to be neutralized by changes in the velocity of the reserve base. For example, reductions in the size of the reserve base could be offset by efforts to increase the amount of loans and deposits sustainable by each dollar of reserves, with the result that bank credit would not be reduced by the reserve contraction. This compensation implies that the Federal funds market can be used as a means of reducing the quantity of idle balances held by the banks or by the public. Refinements of this argument involve the questions of whether this effect is stable enough to be negated by the careful application of additional doses of monetary policy (e.g., the use of a greater volume of open market operations) and whether in that case the Federal Reserve would be willing to apply such additional pressure, knowing that large purchases or sales of securities or large changes in interest rates could destabilize the government bond markets.

In order to be able to sort through the issues raised by these conflicting points of view, one must first construct a thorough description of the market itself. Chapter I of this study is addressed to that point. First it reviews the history of the market in order to discover the reasons for the existence of an interbank lending market of the particular type actually prevailing. It shows that these reasons are not only economic in nature; they involve institutional and political issues as well. Then it examines the mechanics of today's market in some detail, with the hope of revealing some clues as to the direction of causation in the market. Who controls the volume of trading in the market? How important is this market in the mix of adjustment processes available to the system? These and related questions are discussed in that section. Next it presents a microeconomic study of the determinants of bank participation. Since only about half of the member banks in the country are known to be market participants, it may be useful to determine the factors that separate the players from the spectators and the borrowers from the lenders (and both from the two-way traders). The final section of Chapter I examines the flows of

funds through different geographic regions and among various classes of
banks.

The second and third chapters isolate the two principal characteristics of the market: the interest rate charged for loans and the total volume of loans. Chapter II discusses the role of the Federal funds interest
rate in the economy through studies of the relationships between that rate
and the prices of substitute goods. Then Chapter III considers the nature
of trading volume: how it is measured and how it should be interpreted.

Part Two (Chapters IV through VII) takes up the problem of relating
the Federal funds market to the transmission of monetary policy. First
Chapter IV discusses the literature by which alternative hypotheses have
been developed. Then Chapter V uses the market analysis developed in
Part One to develop an explicit model of the Federal funds market as part
of a full model of the U.S. economy. The function of that model is to describe the channels through which monetary policies are transmitted and to
provide a vehicle for testing the role of the funds market in shaping
those channels. The formal testing of the alternative hypotheses is done
in Chapter VI, through econometric estimation of the parameters of the
model and through computer simulation of its properties. A summary of the
market and its role in the policy process is presented in the concluding
chapter.

PART ONE. THE FEDERAL FUNDS MARKET

Chapter One. Structure of the Market

Institutional Development

The <u>Federal Reserve Act</u> provides for a system of reserves wherein the district Federal Reserve Banks serve as demand depositories for the member banks.[1] The reserve account of each member is thus an active account, used for general check clearing and for various business transactions by the bank. Perhaps the crucial distinction held by these reserve balances is that they are designated as immediate credit items; a draft against a reserve account may be presented at a Federal Reserve Bank for immediate payment. Most other types of drafts may be cleared only for deferred credit of one or two days. Clearly, a bank which borrows money for one day will require an immediate credit instrument.

While the form of the transaction is a product of our unique institutional framework, the need for an interbank lending market is derived from imperfections in the banks' market structure. Not only are there severe geographic limitations on the market served by any particular bank, but also the desirability of establishing a continuing customer relationship with a single bank reduces the degree of competitive shopping for bank services.[2] These phenomena can lead to a situation in which some banks will be faced with heavy demands on their funds while other banks, even those in the same geographic area, might have large volumes of funds for which they can find no profitable outlet.

---

1. "The required balance carried by a member bank with a Federal reserve bank may, under the regulations and subject to such penalties as may be described by the Board of Governors of the Federal Reserve System, be checked against and withdrawn by such member bank for the purpose of meeting existing liabilities." 38 Stat. 251; 12 USC 221, Section 19, paragraph 6.

2. For a thorough discussion of this problem, see Donald R. Hodgman, <u>Commercial Bank Loan and Investment Policy</u> (Champaign, Illinois: University of Illinois, 1963); and Comptroller of the Currency, <u>Studies in Banking Competition and the Banking Structure</u> (Washington, 1966).

The manner in which this instability is resolved will depend partly on
banks' expectations of how long the circumstances will persist. Because of
brokerage and other transaction costs and because of the risk of changes in
interest rates, an investor normally will desire to acquire an instrument
whose maturity date most closely coincides with his expectation of the
length of time his funds will be available. This coincidence enables him
to avoid the costs of multiple transactions while buying short-term instruments, or of liquidating long-term instruments in uncertain secondary markets. Borrowers similarly might minimize costs by selling instruments
whose maturity coincides with their shortage of funds.

Here the peculiarities of the Federal Reserve Act again come into play.
The reserve requirements of member banks can be met by maintaining an average balance over a one-week period ending on Wednesday. At the conclusion
of the week, any shortage of reserves will result in a sizable penalty,
and any excess will result in an opportunity cost which cannot be re-
covered. This creates an incentive for banks to exchange reserves among
themselves wherever possible in order to eliminate any difference between
required and actual reserves. Thus the reserve system combines with an
imperfect market structure to create an environment for an interbank market
in Federal Reserve funds.

A bank with a temporary excess in its reserve position actually has a
number of possible means of converting its non-earning assets into earning
assets with only a minimal loss of liquidity. These instruments make up
the so-called money market: Treasury bills and other short-term government
obligations, loans to security dealers or brokers, commercial paper, acceptances, Euro-dollar balances, or loans of Federal funds. The choice of
a particular investment will be a function of relative yields and maturity
options. On the other side of the market the alternatives are somewhat
different. A bank with a temporary shortage of funds may sell any of the
above instruments, but only to the extent that they reside in the bank's
present portfolio. It may, however, buy (i.e., borrow) Federal funds without practical limit. In addition, the bank has the option of borrowing
through the discount window of the Federal Reserve.

The implication of these catalogues is that to the borrower Federal
funds will be a close substitute for the discount window; but to the lender
the closest substitute will be Treasury bills. In order for the funds market to flourish, it must be made in some sense "less expensive" than the

discount window while at the same time made more attractive to lenders
than other money market instruments.

Origins. These circumstances first came together during the recession
of 1921.[1] A large volume of excess reserves accumulated throughout the
country in the second quarter of that year, while some New York banks were
still facing strong enough demands to be borrowing regularly from the discount window. Growing pressures from the New York Fed to reduce this
steady borrowing increased its cost, inducing these banks to search for an
alternative source of short-term funds. Finding other banks with idle
funds, the New York banks simply matched up individual supplies and demands
and traded reserve balances. As Bernice Turner recalled those days a few
years later,

> Some of the leading bankers met informally and discussed the
> problem. They acted on the suggestion that those banks which were
> in debt to the Federal Reserve bank should purchase the excess bal-
> ances of the other banks. This was done by trading Federal reserve
> checks. The bank with the long position at the Federal reserve bank
> would hand to the bank with the short position a check on its excess
> balances. The bank with the short position would use this check to
> pay off its borrowings at the Federal reserve bank. In payment for
> the Funds, the bank with the short position would issue its check
> on the Federal reserve bank for a like amount plus one day's inter-
> est, but the selling bank would not make immediate use of this check;
> instead, it would allow the check to be passed through clearing the
> following morning. In this way, it became possible for the bank
> that was not in debt to realize on these temporary balances until
> it could place its surplus in a safe loan. The rate at which these
> first sales of Federal Funds were made was three-quarters of one per
> cent below the rediscount rate.[2]

---

1. For an excellent treatment of the history of this market, see Parker B. Willis, The Federal Funds Market: Its Origin and Development
(Third Edition; Federal Reserve Bank of Boston, 1968). The interbank lending markets which preceded the Federal funds market, including those which
prevailed under the National Banking System, are discussed in L.L. Watkins,
Bankers' Balances (Chicago: A.W. Shaw, 1929), chapter seven. A good ref-
erence for interbank relationships in the formative years of the Federal
Reserve System is Charles O. Hardy, Credit Policies of the Federal Reserve
System (Washington: Brookings, 1932). Two other standard works on the
relationship of the central bank to the money markets in those years are
Lauchlin Currie, The Supply and Control of Money in the United States
(Boston: Harvard College, 1934); and Winfield W. Riefler, Money Rates and
Money Markets in the United States (New York: Harper and Brothers, 1930).
The aim of the present chapter is not to present a history of these
subjects, but rather to indicate the range of developments which combined
to enhance market growth.

2. The Federal Fund Market (New York: Prentice-Hall, 1931), pp. 18-
19.

At that time, the "rediscount" rate was 6% in New York, and discounts on
short-term government securities were hovering around 5%.[1] A funds rate of
5 1/4% improved the position of both buyers and sellers.

During the 1920's, the funds market evolved much as any primitive market system would. The initial system of barter, in which banks wishing to
buy or sell funds would seek out others with opposite positions in like
amounts, gradually was replaced by the emergence of brokers. The first
brokers were companies which dealt primarily in bankers' acceptances and
maintained non-member accounts at the Federal Reserve Bank of New York for
clearing purposes.[2] They were in an ideal position to serve as intermediaries for funds transfers, thereby enabling the market to grow rapidly during that decade. For example, an acceptance house could acquire a reserve
balance by selling bills or government securities to the New York Fed and
taking payment in the form of a Federal Reserve draft. These funds then
could be sold to banks with reserve shortages. In this manner a pool of
funds developed, creating a market in which bankers could more easily even
out their reserve positions.

It is somewhat surprising that the Federal Reserve System issued no
statements of policy regarding the funds market during the first several
years of its growth. In fact, to this day the official statements of the
Board of Governors have been limited to rulings as to the manner in which
transactions are to be reported. This in spite of the fact that the funds
market may reduce the effectiveness of discount policy by permitting banks
to avoid surveillance while borrowing reserves. Furthermore, during the
Twenties the operation of the funds market sharply reduced the earnings of
the Federal Reserve Bank of New York. In the days prior to rapid growth
of the Federal debt, a growth which enabled the Federal Reserve System to
realize enormous incomes on its own holdings of government securities, the
Reserve Banks were forced to get along mainly on the income from their
loans and discounts to member banks. By 1920 such income in New York had
grown to nearly $50 million per year, representing 83% of the total income

---

1. Board of Governors of the Federal Reserve System (cited hereinafter
as "Board of Governors"), Banking and Monetary Statistics (Washington,
1943), pp. 440, 460.

2. Willis, The Federal Funds Market, p. 6.

of the Federal Reserve Bank of New York.[1] In the following year, the year in which the funds market began to supplant the discount window as a source of short-term balances, income from discounted bills at the New York Fed fell to $31 million. By the next year it was down to $4 million, and it never again rose above $12.5 million. Not all of this decline, of course, can be attributed to the growth of the funds market. But taking estimates of average daily volume of trading in the funds market[2] and multiplying them by the prevailing discount rate, assuming that all transactions in this market otherwise would have gone through the discount window, yields the following estimates of income lost by the Federal Reserve:

```
1922   $2.3 million   (or 12% of actual total income)
1925    4.9 million   (48%)
1928    7.9 million   (43%)
```

Without question the total loss during the decade was large enough to create financial difficulties for the Federal Reserve. In three of the first ten years of the market's existence the New York Fed was unable to pay dividends without drawing on its surplus.[3]

Nonetheless the System seemed to view the funds market favorably even during that first decade, initiating what is now a tradition of freedom from regulation. Perhaps the major factor inhibiting growth of the market was the provincialism (or what Bernice Turner called the "keenness and integrity"[4]) of the New York bankers, who adhered tightly to a policy of not dealing with any out-of-town banks, extending the ban even to their own correspondents.[5] This policy was not completely abandoned until some thirty years after the New York market began. And because there were not enough large banks in other financial centers to establish regional markets, trading in Federal funds was effectively restricted to New York and a few other large cities.

By 1929 this New York market seemed to be firmly established: some forty banks and ten acceptance houses were actively trading Federal funds,

---

1. Lawrence E. Clark, Central Banking Under the Federal Reserve System (New York: MacMillan and Company, 1935), p. 109.

2. Willis, The Federal Funds Market, p. 12.

3. Clark, p. 108.

4. Turner, p. 85.

5. Board of Governors, The Federal Funds Market (Washington, 1959), pp. 25-26.

with the daily volume peaking in the neighborhood of $250 million.[1] Then
with the "great contraction," the funds market almost disappeared for a
full decade. Every bank had excess reserves, and the demand for bank credit was insufficient to attract funds into the financial centers. Because
the funds market relies on market imperfections which cause some banks to
have reserve shortages while other have surpluses, it would seem that it
could thrive only when Federal Reserve policy and economic conditions in
general are neither extremely easy nor extremely tight. In practice, as
will be shown in detail later, conditions are not likely ever to become
tight enough to dry up the supply of reserve funds, but, during the Thir-
ties, conditions definitely did become loose enough to dry up the demand.

When the United States entered World War II, there was an immediate
and sharp increase in credit demands, tightening reserve positions and re-
activating the money market. Furthermore, the war itself was financed
largely by the sale of short-term government securities. Movement by banks
in and out of positions in government securities, settling transactions in
reserve funds, caused wide fluctuations in reserve positions and further
stimulated Federal funds activity.[2] This relationship between securities
and reserves in bank asset portfolios is an important linkage to under-
stand, both because of its effect on the volume of funds trading during
periods of major Treasury financing and because of its effect on interest
rate differentials in the money market. This latter relation will be
examined at length below.[3]   .

Postwar Development. At this point, the Federal funds market was still
the special province of the New York banker. Then in 1950 there occurred
a technological advance in banking which helped transform the funds market
into a national market, the sort of market which eventually would have a
major impact on the transmission of monetary policy. This advance was the
bank wire, a teletype service linking banks in major cities around the
country. Through the use of this wire service, it became quite easy for a
bank wishing to buy or sell funds to contact a large number of other banks
cheaply and quickly, avoiding the need for a broker and increasing the
relative advantage of dealing with banks in distant cities.

1. Ibid., p. 23.
2. Ibid., pp. 38-39.
3. Chapter II, pp. 48-59.

A number of other structural and legal developments combined in the postwar period to enhance the growth of the market. Reduction, between 1937 and 1950, of the maximum credit deferment on items cleared through the Federal Reserve from eight days to two days caused Federal Reserve float to fluctuate more than it once did, increasing the volatility of bank reserve positions.[1] Since on any given day transportation peculiarities and other delays will cause many checks to be cleared after (or perhaps before) the automatic deferred credit date set by the Federal Reserve, a large and widely fluctuating volume of float is created. As the periods established for clearing checks have been reduced, these fluctuations have become larger and more sudden. They shift reserves among banks in a pattern out of phase with deposit shifts and increase the demand for Federal funds trading.

A most revealing development leading to market growth--revealing in the sense of yielding insights into the way markets in fact grow in our economy--is the 1963 ruling by James Saxon as Comptroller of the Currency. The national banking laws provide that "no National banking association shall at any time be indebted, or in any way liable, to an amount exceeding the amount of its capital stock...plus fifty percent of the amount of its unimpaired surplus fund..."[2] This rule sets an upper limit on the amount that a bank can borrow at any given time. The additional, tighter restriction is made that the "total obligations to any National banking association of any person, copartnership, association, or corporation shall at no time exceed ten per centum of its unimpaired surplus funds."[3] This well-known "ten percent" rule sets an absolute upper limit on the amount that a bank can lend to a single borrower. These limits are effective for almost all types of loans but are especially important when applied to Federal funds which, because of their very short maturities, must be handled in large blocks in order to be profitable. When the legal lending limits were enforced, the maximum amounts which small banks could lend were far smaller than the minimum amounts which could profitably be handled. The exclusion of the great majority of banks from market participation placed a severe damper on the total volume of transactions.

---

1. Board of Governors, The Federal Funds Market, p. 36.

2. Federal Reserve Act, Section 13, paragraph 9.

3. Ibid., appendix of related statutes, 12 USC 84 (R.S. 5200), p. 129.

It is obvious to any observer or participant in the money market that
an interbank Federal funds transaction is a loan from one bank to another.
The Federal Reserve Board first ruled in September, 1928 that a transfer
of Federal funds "clearly is a temporary loan...and the resulting liability
should be treated as money borrowed."[1] In February, 1930, it reaffirmed
that ruling: "transactions of this kind are manifestly temporary loans."[2]
This decision went unquestioned until Comptroller Saxon appeared and declared that

> ...when a national bank purchases Federal Reserve funds from another
> bank, the transaction ordinarily takes the form of a transfer from
> the seller's account in the Federal Reserve Bank to the buyer's
> account therein, payment to be made by the purchaser, usually with
> a specified fee. The transaction does not give rise to an obliga-
> tion of the buyer subject to the lending or borrowing limit as de-
> fined in 12 U.S.C. 82 [quoted above, p. 9] but is to be considered
> a purchase and sale of such funds.[3]

Such an unsubtle subterfuge brought an angry blast from the Legislative
Reference Section of the Library of Congress. In appraising this and
several other rulings by Mr. Saxon, they argued that

> The Comptroller is unable to distinguish between the more liberal
> standard, or implied powers doctrine, of interpretation which has been
> employed to deduce the broad measure of authority exercisable by or-
> dinary business corporations and the very limited scope of authority
> available to national banks...a researcher who has encountered neither
> legal precedents nor legislative records favorable to his rulings is
> at a loss to understand the boundless confidence with which he presents
> conclusions as having been accepted by a preponderant weight of author-
> ity.[4]

Nonetheless, the Comptroller's ruling that loans of Federal funds are
not loans at all has been accepted by all concerned parties as the appropriate concept. The Federal Reserve, while continuing to admit that funds
transactions "are really loans from one bank to another with a one-day
maturity,"[5] now uses the terms "purchase" and "sale" almost exclusively,

---

1. Federal Reserve Bulletin, XIV (September, 1928), 656 .

2. Ibid., XVI (February, 1930), 81.

3. Legislative Reference Section of the Library of Congress, "Independent Appraisal of Certain Rulings of the Comptroller of the Currency"
(Washington, 1965), p. [3.

4. Ibid., p. [2 .

5. Dorothy M. Nichols, "Marketing Money: How 'Smaller' Banks Buy and
Sell Federal Funds," Federal Reserve Bank of Chicago Business Conditions,
August, 1965, p. 8.

call reports included, and it has implicitly accepted the absence of any limits on the maximum size of such transactions. In this manner, the Federal funds market has been enabled to expand to include, potentially, all commercial banks.

Operation of the Mature Market

As the preceding section has indicated, the funds market today is available virtually to any bank desiring to participate, thanks to a variety of economic, institutional, and legal developments favorable to its growth. Although actual growth has lagged behind potential growth, the market today is very widespread. Until recently, the Federal Reserve had made only sporadic attempts to monitor the extent or even the nature of bank participation in the funds market, so that any estimates of growth must be highly tentative. Perhaps the best guess would be that about half of the banks which are members of the Federal Reserve System do at least some trading. Adding in the number of nonmembers who trade funds through their correspondents would bring the total number of participants to around 3,500. This figure is somewhat above Parker Willis' estimate of 3,000,[1] but it probably does not overstate the situation. The great majority of these participants enter the market only occasionally; most of them did not participate at all prior to the Sixties.

The total volume of trading is not much easier to estimate. There are numerous problems even in deciding how volume of trading should be measured, and, as will be discussed at length below, many analysts still are indifferent as to the magnitude of total volume.[2] However, it is clear that at least four to five billion dollars change hands on an average day. The actual total may be much higher. Perhaps it would be useful to compare this figure with the volumes traded daily in other money market and related instruments, as shown for a representative month in Table 1.

In that same month (December, 1969), excess reserves in the entire System averaged $257 million. There can be no question that the Federal funds market has assumed dimensions capable of exerting strong leverage between policy actions and changes in reserve positions. The nature of this leverage perhaps can best be understood through a close look at the mechanics

1. Willis, The Federal Funds Market, p. 42.
2. See Chapter III, pp. 62-67.

Table 1. Trading Volume in Money Market Instruments. Daily Average, December, 1969

Instrument	Millions of Dollars
Federal funds	10,100
Treasury bills	1,981
Federal agency securities	256
Other short-term governments	181
Bankers' acceptances	268
Negotiable CD's	5
Borrowing from discount window	1,086

Source: All figures except those for the discount window are from Jimmie
    R. Monhollon (ed.), Instruments of the Money Market, 2nd Ed., (Federal
    Reserve Bank of Richmond, 1970), p. 10. Discount volume is average
    outstanding borrowed reserves during the month, from the Federal Re-
    serve Bulletin, LVI, (February, 1970), A6. It is not strictly compar-
    able to the other figures.

of the market, at the ways in which several billion dollars are bought and
sold each day.

The Players. There are basically four types of participants in the
market. First, there are the sellers. These are medium- or small-sized
banks, often located in suburban areas or small towns, which enter the market primarily to get rid of temporary excesses in their reserve positions.
They sometimes will purchase funds, but most banks in this group exhibit a
strong reluctance to borrow money from any source. These banks make up by
far the largest of the four groups. Most of their sales are made to the
intermediaries. This second group consists of fairly large banks located
primarily in reserve cities around the country; they stand ready to buy
any amount of funds offered to them by their customer banks (the banks
which use them as a principal correspondent). The intermediaries normally
will maintain a deficit in their basic reserve position corresponding to
their expected purchases of funds. That is, their basic reserve balance
at the Federal Reserve will be maintained at a level below their expected
reserve requirement, the banks making up the difference by buying reserves
offered by their correspondents. Any differences between their purchases
and their deliberate deficit are resolved by sales made to their own correspondents, usually a New York bank. Those correspondents make up the
third major group, the buyers. They actively seek purchases of funds, in

contrast to the intermediaries which passively accept offers to sell. The
buyers almost always run quite large basic deficits and use the funds market as a permanent source of lendable funds. They largely determine the
interest rates at which funds will be traded around the country. Buyers
are a rather small group of very large banks, and they account for most of
the total volume of trading each day. Finally, there are the balancers.
This fourth group consists of medium- to large-sized banks which, because
of limited size or sheer disinclination, do not operate a volume of correspondent business big enough to enable them to serve as intermediaries
but whose management is sophisticated enough to keep a tight rein on the
bank's daily reserve position. These banks then balance their position
through the Federal funds market, buying or selling as their figures dictate. On some occasions they may even buy and sell on the same day, as
their estimates of their reserve flows change with new information.

The flow of funds among these groups runs generally from small banks
to larger banks and from rural areas to urban areas to reserve cities and
ultimately to New York. The hub of the market is still the city of New
York. There the rates are determined and, through the rates, the volume
of trading. The New York buyers actually use a number of different markets
to purchase their Federal funds. The simplest of these is the intracity
market, in which one bank calls other banks by telephone to try to locate
a seller. Similarly, a bank can use the bank wire, or again, the telephone, to contact its counterparts in other cities. Today this second type
of market is probably the largest, reflecting the strength of the correspondent system. But until some ten years ago, the most popular means of
trading funds was through a small number of non-bank brokerage firms. During the late Forties, a single funds broker--Garvin, Bantel and Co., the
forerunner of the Garvin Bantel Corporation--reportedly handled nearly 80%
of all Federal funds transfers.[1] Because of the development of correspondent services and the introduction of the bank wire, this percentage fell
considerably during the Fifties and the Sixties. Most banks prefer to control the sources and dispositions of their funds, rather than to work
through the impersonal and therefore somewhat riskier world of the brokerage houses. By 1957, Garvin Bantel was handling about 50% of the transfers, a proportion representing at that time more than a billion dollars

---

1. Willis, The Federal Funds Market, p. 44.

per day; but the firm's share and brokers' shares in general have continued to drop.[1]

Federal funds brokers, perhaps because of the keen competition from
correspondent bankers, seldom charge for their services. They act solely
as clearing houses, bringing together buyers and sellers. In return, they
expect to receive indirect compensation in the form of other types of
brokerage business from the banks involved. In a few cases in which a
small bank lacks the ability to supply such business, a spread of perhaps
one-eighth of a percentage point may be charged.[2]

There is yet another type of participant in the funds market: the
government securities dealer. Several non-bank corporations currently
maintain clearing facilities with the Federal Reserve Bank of New York and
settle their transactions in short-term government securities through Federal Reserve drafts. This however is a completely distinct operation from
the proper Federal funds market, and it is of no interest to the present
study. All figures on trading volume with which we are now concerned exclude trades made with securities dealers and other non-bank companies.[3]

The Play. Regardless of the manner in which a bank becomes involved
in the funds market, the most serious mechanical problem it faces is that
of forecasting its reserve position. The procedures established by the
Federal Reserve Banks are such that the member bank cannot know its position precisely until it is too late to make further adjustments. Until
1968, the procedures were as follows. Each member bank was required to
maintain a reserve balance averaging an amount equal to or greater than a
fixed percentage of its average daily deposits. Reserve city banks were
permitted to average deposits and reserves over one-week periods ending
each Wednesday; country banks were allowed a two-week period. Then effective September 12, 1968, the Board of Governors amended the regulations in
three ways. First, all member banks regardless of class were to be put on

---

1. Ibid.

2. J.S.G. Wilson, Monetary Policy and the Development of Money Markets
(London: George Allen and Unwin, 1966), p. 161.

3. For a thorough discussion of the role of the securities dealer, see
Frederick Gidge, "Billion Dollar Specialty: Security Dealer Clearance,"
Burroughs Clearing House, XLVIII (August, 1964), 44-45; Willis, The Federal
Funds Market, 20-24; and Allan H. Meltzer and G.v.d. Linde, A Study of the
Dealer Market for Federal Government Securities, materials prepared for the
Joint Economic Committee, U.S. Congress (86th Cong., 2d sess., 1960).

a one-week computation period. Second, the deposits on which current reserve requirements were to be based would be those held by the bank two
weeks previously. Third, small excesses or deficiencies could be carried
over to the following week.[1]

Consider then the following case study, using actual figures for a
country bank on November 24, 1965. The problem faced by the bank was to
calculate its deposits as of the opening of the business day and to forecast its reserve balance as of the close of the business day. Any discrep-
ancy between its reserve requirement for the day and its projected reserve
balance then might be resolved in the funds market.

First, the bank calculated its reserve requirement for the day on the
basis of its known deposits as of the opening of business. For the day in
question, a Wednesday, the bank held net demand deposits of $27,140,000
and time deposits of $21,467,000. Its required reserve was 12% of the for-
mer plus 4% of the latter, or $4,116,000. The bank had on hand currency
and coin totalling $1,335,000, so it would need by the end of the day a
balance in its account at the Fed of $2,781,000.

The larger job was to forecast its probable balance at the end of the
day. The bank received early that morning a statement from its Reserve
Bank giving the bank's actual closing balance from the previous day. To
this figure would now be appended the day's activity on the account. This
activity could not be predicted with complete certainty, but could be estimated in the following way.

1. Deduct all incoming cash letters (checks drawn on this bank and
being cleared against it through the Reserve System) and Federal Reserve
drafts written by bank officials the previous day, if they are likely to be
debited against the reserve balance today. These items can be a major
source of uncertainty when drafts are cleared against the bank at an unexpected rate. A clear reading of the timing of major debits is essential
if the bank is to balance its account closely. In our example, nearly a
million dollars is involved.

2. Settle any outstanding transfers of Federal funds. Here the bank
had made a loan of $1.5 million on November 23; that amount would be re-
stored to the reserve balance today.

---

1. Board of Governors, Regulation D: Reserves of Member Banks, 12
CFR 204, as amended effective September 12, 1968.

3. Subtract any scheduled withdrawals from the Treasury's Tax and Loan account. Corporations and other employers who collect withholding tax and other taxes from their employees deposit the money in a designated commercial bank. The bank credits the Tax and Loan account of the U.S. Treasury, and the money is held in the account until it is needed by the Treasury to meet disbursements. Withdrawals are made at irregular intervals, but only with advance notice to the banks involved. At our sample bank, this account will vary from $200,000 to $1,000,000 generally rising early in each month and falling toward the end. The bank had been notified that $109,487.53 would be withdrawn on November 24; this amount therefore was subtracted from the estimated reserve balance.

4. Deduct any currency and coin orders. Cash requirements for bank operations are satisfied by shipments from the Federal Reserve, with payment made by a direct debit against the bank's account.

5. Add in any deferred credit items. When checks are cleared through the Federal Reserve System, the bank submitting items for credit is notified as to when it will be given credit. If the Fed expects to be able to clear the item in two days, it will notify the bank that its balance will be credited at that time. On each business day, the bank's reserve account will be increased by the amount of these items which previously had been deferred but which now have become due. These amounts are known with certainty.

6. Add or subtract any transfers from or to correspondent accounts. These transfers reflect existing agreements to maintain balances at correspondent banks at certain levels. For example, this bank tried to maintain a balance of $900,000 at a large Chicago bank. On the day in question, its opening balance there was about $1.2 million. This imbalance now would be corrected by transferring $300,000 from the correspondent account to the reserve account.

When placed on the bank's daily work sheet, these figures appeared as shown below.

	closing balance at the Fed	$2,565,974.01
(1)	adverse clearings and drafts	- 996,959.99
	opening balance today	1,569,014.02
(2)	settlement of funds loans	+1,500,000.00
(3)	withdrawals from Tax and Loan	- 109,487.53
(4)	coin orders	- 47,000.00
(5)	deferred credit--one day	+ 126,544.37
	deferred credit--two days	+ 268,097.03
(6)	transfers	+ 300,000.00
	estimated closing balance	$3,607,167.89

This figure exceeded the bank's requirement (shown above to be $2,781,000) by $826,000. In addition to this excess, the bank had accumulated excess reserves of $395,000 over the previous thirteen days of its computation period, for a total surplus of $1,221,000. Assuming that the auditing department had done its work well, the bank could now lend $1.2 million over the Thanksgiving holiday, leaving itself with excess reserves averaging only $1500 per day, or about one-twentieth of one percent of its average legal reserve requirement for the period.

This example raises some interesting points. First, it appears that the 1968 amendment to Regulation D, permitting banks to calculate their reserve requirement on their deposits of a fortnight ago, is not so major a factor in reducing the uncertainty in reserve accounting as a surface examination might lead one to believe. As seen in the example, the practice prior to passage of that amendment was to base the requirement on the deposits as of the opening of business each day (which is to say, the deposits as of the close of business the previous day). This figure is known with the same certainty as is the deposit level held two weeks earlier. Therefore, the change in the regulation makes no difference whatsoever in the exactitude with which the reserve calculations can be carried out.

If this amendment were to have any effect here, it would be to affect the expected difference between the reserve balance and the requirement on the remaining days of the computation period. However, by fixing the level of the requirement without altering the determination of the reserve balance, this new rule could even increase this expected difference. Suppose, for example, that a bank experiences a regular intramonthly cycle in its deposit level. Before September, 1968, its deposits and reserves would fluctuate simultaneously; now they will move against each other. The bank will face its highest reserve requirements at times when its deposits and hence its reserve balance are at an ebb, and conversely. This amendment, therefore, is not likely to affect significantly the demand by the banking system for means of adjusting its short-run reserve imbalances.

A second observation raised by the example is that banks very much smaller than this one would not appear to be in a position to profit from regular trading in Federal funds. If the figures cited can be taken as typical, a bank with deposits of $50 million or so might reasonably expect its normal reserve flows to provide it with temporary excesses or deficien-

cies of one or two million dollars, while a bank with $20 million in de-
posits would see that magnitude of imbalance much less frequently. And
certainly if a ten-million-dollar bank wants to participate regularly it
will have to try to negotiate transfers in the range of $100,000 or so.
Suppose the interest rate on funds is 5%. Then an overnight loan of
$100,000 will gross only $13.89, an amount which probably is insufficient
to cover the costs of the phone calls, letters, and telegrams needed to
consummate the transfer, much less the cost of forecasting a daily reserve
position. It is an interesting aspect of the funds market that a large
number of very small banks do participate and that they do make loans of
$100,000 or less, even when the interest rate to be obtained is well below
5%. The nature of this involvement will be detailed below.[1]

A third observation is that a bank must use fairly sophisticated management techniques in order to play the market as closely as it was played
in the example. The net yield to the bank from loans of Federal funds
over that two-week computation period was on the order of $1,000 to $2,000.
If the bank had not sold funds in the market, its excess reserves would
have earned no interest. However, the bank was risking a reserve deficiency. At the end of the period it had an accumulated excess of just
$21,000 in a reserve account that was fluctuating by millions of dollars
every day. Unfortunately the costs of reserve deficiencies are somewhat
ambiguous. Officially the Federal Reserve banks will permit members to
run occasional deficiencies of as much as two percent of the average requirement with no penalty. Unofficially they normally permit larger
shortages to occur, subject only to a waived penalty. And even in the
rare instance when a penalty is assessed, it amounts only to "a rate of 2
per cent per annum above the lowest rate applicable to borrowings by each
member bank from its Federal Reserve Bank...".[2] This "penalty" is in fact
a lending rate which may be even less than the bank's own prime rate. The
true penalty costs are subjective, arising either from voluntary reluctance
to incur shortages or from unofficial surveillance procedures practiced by
the Reserve bank. Whatever the nature of these costs, they generally are
perceived by the banking community to be sufficiently high to prevent recurring shortages. Banks which lack complete confidence in their reserve
forecasts are unlikely to be active traders of Federal funds.

1. See p. .22.

2. Board of Governors, Regulation D.

This case study concerned itself only with the problems of a bank in
the fourth group of our classification of participants, the "balancers."
The problems of the sellers-only are quite similar, but in the case of the
intermediaries and the buyers, the operation becomes a bit more complex.
Take the case of the "A" National Bank (ANB), a large intermediary in the
Midwest which regularly buys from and sells to more than one hundred correspondent banks; on an average day in 1965, between sixty and seventy of
those banks were disposing of a total of about $50 million through ANB and
were borrowing approximately $7 million. The bank borrows amounts as
small as $100,000 and as large as might be offered. In addition, it
stands ready to lend to preferred banks up to 50% of the borrower's capital and surplus. It maintains a basic reserve deficit of about $20 mil-
lion and disposes of any excess reserve funds by selling to major banks
throughout the country. It claims to operate this brokerage business
purely as a service to its correspondents, making up a net operating loss
in the funds market by attracting additional deposit balances from correspondents.

The intermediary computes its reserve position in the same way as the
balancer, except that it has to keep running tabs on a large number of
transfers of funds throughout the day. While the auditing department is
calculating the reserve balance, the money desk in the investments department is buying and selling vast sums of reserve funds. By definition, the
intermediary has no control over the volume of its purchases; it accepts
whatever its correspondents offer. The problem faced by the reserve officer is simply to balance his account as closely as possible, once he can
get a clear reading of the volume of funds coming into the bank through
the market. In that respect, there is no real difference between this
type of operation and that of the smaller banks.

Finally we come to the buyers. Up to this point, the market lacks
volition; the sellers and the balancers enter the market only as their reserve positions and the relative attractiveness of funds permit, and the
intermediaries simply accept funds offered to them, offering whatever interest rate is prevailing in the central money markets and disposing of
any excess purchases in that same market. Meanwhile, the buyers are in a
sense controlling this activity. In New York, Chicago, San Francisco, and
a small number of other reserve cities the major banks are making decisions
each day to determine the volume of reserve funds which they need to

attract in order to satisfy the short-term demands for credit which they
face from security brokers and dealers as well as from other borrowers.
These decisions collectively determine the interest rate which will prevail for the morning. For example, the officer at the money desk at ANB
will make a number of phone calls to various points around the country
each morning, asking funds buyers for their offering rates and their assess-
ments of the current tone of the market. He then knows pretty well the
rate at which he will be able to unload funds later in the day, and this
information will determine the rate that he offers to his own correspondents. This process is repeated throughout the market. If it turns out--
by eleven o'clock or noon--that the buyers' rate decisions are attracting
a different volume of funds than was anticipated, the rate will begin to
move in one direction or the other. If the supply at any given moment becomes too plentiful for existing credit demands, the rate can very quickly
fall to near zero. Federal funds are not a storable commodity.

This discussion of the operation of the funds market would not be complete without some mention of the manner in which the actual transfers of
funds are made. Recall the case study given above. The officers of our
country bank, having decided to sell $1.2 million in the Federal funds mar-
ket, had two phone calls to make. First, they called ANB and asked what
interest rate it was offering at the moment. 4 1/8% being acceptable to
them, they offered the funds and ANB accepted the loan. It was implicitly
understood, though not even mentioned at the time, that the loan was to
mature on the next business day, in this case the Friday after the Thanks-
giving holiday. Next the selling bank called the Federal Reserve Bank of
Chicago and instructed it to transfer the funds from its own account to
that of ANB. On Friday, ANB would reverse the procedure, returning the
funds to the lender. Later, letters would be sent to confirm the phone
calls; these letters would then serve as the official loan agreement. The
interest payment for the loan, $275.00, would be made by a credit to the
seller's account at ANB.

Funds can be transferred by an even simpler means, which is used most
frequently when nonmember banks wish to get involved. Banks which are not
members of the Federal Reserve System normally maintain a major portion of
their state reserve requirement in the form of a demand deposit balance at
a reserve city bank which is a member of the System. This account is used

for check-clearing purposes, just as if the city correspondent were a
Reserve Bank to its correspondent. Now if the nonmember wishes to sell
"Federal funds," it can call this depository and ask it to transfer some
amount from its deposit account to another account, "bills payable." This
action creates a loan from the nonmember to its correspondent, usually
with interest being paid at the going rate on Federal funds. The city
bank must make the assumption that it would lose the deposit anyway if it
did not perform this service; otherwise it is in effect paying interest on
a demand deposit account, an illegal act under Regulation Q. Since the
"bills payable" account is a liability which does not carry a reserve requirement, a fraction of the amount of the loan becomes excess reserves to
the city bank. Any bank which regularly can convert part of its deposits
into some form of borrowing can lower its effective reserve requirement,
freeing a portion of its asset portfolio for profitable investment. Furthermore, if it is true that the "borrowing" bank would have lost the deposit had it not agreed to the loan, then in a sense it has gained reserves which are available for investment in the funds market or elsewhere.
It is probably true that most of this type of activity never shows up in
the statistics on the funds market but is confined to the figures on
"other borrowing." Federal Reserve officials have chosen tacitly to accept this behavior as legitimate probably on the grounds that prohibiting
it would lead only to any number of other forms of transfer in circumven-
tion of the regulations. No figures exist to measure its extent or its
importance in the money market.

Determinants of Bank Participation

Perhaps the most detailed study of the determinants of bank participation in this market was made by the Federal Reserve Bank of Atlanta in
1967.[1] Questionnaires were sent to all member banks in the district (and
were completed by more than 98% of them) not only to discover which banks
were currently trading what volume of funds, but also to determine why some
banks liked the market while others stayed aloof; why some banks would lend

---

1. For detailed descriptions of that study, see Brandt and Crowe,
"Trading in Federal Funds by Banks in the Southeast," and "The Federal
Funds Market in the Southeast," Federal Reserve Bank of Atlanta Monthly Re-
view, LIII (January, 1968), 7-13; and Boughton, "The Effect of an Active
Market in Federal Funds on the Transmission of Monetary Policy," pp. 36-60.

funds but refuse to borrow them; and a number of related questions. Since
one finding of the survey was that the behavior of Atlanta District banks
with respect to the funds market appeared to be quite similar to that found
in other parts of the country by other surveys, it may be interesting to
summarize the principal discoveries here.

Certainly the most obvious bank characteristic to examine as a possible
explanator of participation in the Federal funds market is size. It is
readily apparent that the bank which can accumulate excess reserves in very
large sums--preferably at least one million dollars in order to gross
$100 or so on a one-day loan--is in a much better position to be able to
cover the fixed costs of transferring funds and to profit from selling
funds. Similarly, the bank which has funds requirements in large quantities will find the Federal funds market a more readily available source
than will the bank with reserve shortages of only a few thousand dollars.
This point, however, should not be overemphasized, for the past several
years have seen a dramatic reduction in minimum trading units, primarily
because of the previously mentioned improvements in wire transfer facilities, other cost reductions, increases in prevailing interest rates, and
the increasing use of the funds market as a "loss leader" by large correspondents in order to attract the demand deposits of small banks. This
last development, in particular, probably explains best why, for example,
a bank with assets of more than $300 million will be found buying and sell-
ing funds in units as small as $25,000. In the Sixth District survey,
two banks reported minimum trading units of $10,000 (loans which even at
6% will yield only $1.67); a dozen banks were making trades of less than
$100,000, and a full 85% of the participants had broken the once-inflexible
floor of one million dollars.

The reduction over time of the minimum trading units, combined with a
gradual relaxation of the rules governing the maximum permissible borrowing and lending relative to each bank's resources and a growing sophistication of small bank management, have led to smaller and smaller participating banks. Of the Sixth District banks which were using the market
prior to 1960, nearly 80% were banks with $100 million or more in total
deposits. In contrast, most banks entering the market for the first time
in recent years have been in the $2-$25 million group, a class of banks
which was scarcely aware of the market's existence a decade ago.

This democratization of the market notwithstanding, large banks still

are more likely to be market participants, and their volume of trading will
be greater than that of their smaller colleagues. This fact is revealed
in two summary statistics:

1. the mean deposit size of participating banks in 1966 was still
   around $60 million, while the figure for inactive banks was about
   $10 million;

2. more than 55% of the variance in trading volume among active banks
   can be explained by bank size alone, and the elasticity of trading
   volume with respect to bank size is about 1.3.[1]

A second likely candidate is the volatility of a bank's total deposits.
At least until recently, most banks found trading in Federal funds to be
profitable only if they had very short-run excesses or deficiencies in
their reserve positions. Otherwise they would do better to place their
assets in longer-maturity instruments with higher yields. Therefore banks
with relatively stable balance sheets would be less likely to engage in
Federal funds trading.

There is very little evidence on this conjecture, largely because the
requisite data are not available. An indirect test was made in the Sixth
District study, in which the district was divided into two areas: a
"heartland," consisting of the inland urban and agricultural region; and
an outer ring, consisting of various resort areas (principally in Florida)
and several port cities (including Savannah and New Orleans). Since those
latter areas are known to attract a large body of fluctuating seasonal
deposits, banks there should be more active in the funds market than banks
located in the heartland. Indeed, while 64% of the outlying banks were
market participants, only 33% of those in the interior could be so classified. This same pattern was found to hold for each local area within the
larger regions. While not an overwhelming piece of evidence, this dis-
covery does support the hypothesis.

---

1. A regression of trading volume on deposit size, using data for
Atlanta District banks in 1966, reveals that

$$\text{VOLUME} = -130.96 + 10.42 \cdot \text{DEPOSITS} \qquad (\bar{R}^2 = .55)$$
$$\phantom{\text{VOLUME} = }(71.89) \quad (0.60)$$

The data are in millions of dollars at annual rates. Volume is the sum of
all purchases and sales of funds. Standard errors are given in parentheses. The elasticity quoted above is obtained by dividing the coefficient
on DEPOSITS by the ratio of the mean values of the dependent and independent variables. An elasticity greater than unity indicates that trading
volume changes more than proportionately to changes in bank size.

A third characteristic linked to the funds market, after the size and volatility of a bank's deposits, is the profitability of the bank. Here a number of forces come into play. Banks which trade Federal funds probably will be watching their reserve positions closely, which requires a degree of alertness and some sophistication. Furthermore, these banks will be watching interest rate, cost, and risk differentials among alternative sources and uses of funds and may be expected to be taking advantage of such differences. Their excess reserves probably will not be so great as those of the non-trader, since the latter is excluding himself from the possibility of utilizing excesses when they occur for short periods. On the other hand, as indicated above, the lack of such temporary excesses or deficiencies may be a significant characteristic of non-traders.

One might reasonably expect those banks which are active in the funds market to be more profitable than other banks. This expectation proved to be wrong for banks in the Sixth District. Whether profitability is measured by the ratio of income to assets or by the ratio of earnings to revenue, the mean ratio for non-participants is significantly higher than that for the active banks, even when the differences are adjusted for differences in the size of the banks. This effect is shown in Table 2.

There are two plausible explanations for this apparent anomaly. The first is that banks which invest in the sale of Federal funds are receiving a lower return on this portion of their assets than they might be able to receive on an instrument of longer maturity. Banks which borrowed Federal funds during 1966 paid dearly for these funds, relative to the discount rate and to the rates, subject to Regulation Q, which they would have had to pay for new deposits. Rates on Federal funds during 1966 were low relative to returns on loans and other short-term investments but were high relative to other borrowing costs. The banks using this market may have been motivated more by expediency than by profit considerations, thereby actually lowering their net earnings. This argument loses its intuitive appeal when one asks whether the participating banks could have cost themselves enough money by trading funds to create the profit differentials cited in Table 2; the Federal funds market simply could not be that important a determinant of bank profitability. A more likely explanation is that banks may be driven into the funds market, particularly as

Table 2. Profit Ratios for Sixth District Member Banks in 1966 Classified by Type of Federal Funds Activity and by Deposit Size

	Mean Profit Ratio[a] for Banks Which		
	Use Both Sides of Market	Use One Side Only	Do Not Use Market
A. Net Current Earnings as Percentage of Total Revenue			
Deposit Size of Banks (Millions of Dollars)			
Less than 5	14%	17%	21%
5 to 25	22	23	25
25 and over	25	29	31
B. Net Income After Taxes as Percentage of Total Assets			
Deposit Size of Banks (Millions of Dollars)			
Less than 5	0.37	0.49	0.73
5 to 25	.69	.73	.79
25 and over	.70	.80	.95

a. F tests performed across each row indicate that the differences between participants and non-participants are significant except for the "5 to 25" classification. Differences between one-way and two-way traders generally are not significant.

Source: "Operating Ratios," Federal Reserve Bank of Atlanta, 1966; internal files containing individual bank data were used for generating the classification for this table.

sellers, by a lack of profitability, caused perhaps by idle funds; the funds market may not create, but may be created by, low profits.

Some evidence for this latter view was provided by the answers given on the survey questionnaire. Fifty-one banks noted that a profit squeeze had been a major factor influencing their initial entry into the market. These profit reductions had been caused mostly by rising interest rates paid on time deposits, rising ratios of time to total deposits, and rising operating costs. Analyzing these responses led to the conclusion that a number of the District's active traders would never have entered the market were it not for these income problems. This group of low-profit banks

probably accounts for the inverse relationship between profits and participation.

A more conventional positive correlation was found between market activity and the growth rate of the bank's assets. One would expect that
the pressures on the asset structure caused by rapid growth, such as reductions in holdings of secondary reserves to facilitate growth in the loan
portfolio, might lead such banks to turn to the funds market as a source
of lendable funds. The Sixth District survey revealed, for example, that
"small" banks (less than $5 million in total deposits) which use the Fed-
eral funds market only for purchasing experienced a 67% increase in loan
volume during the period examined (1966). Banks of that size which did
not use the market showed a growth rate of 24%. This finding certainly
corroborates the "growth pains" theory of market development.

Table 3. Market Participation by Urban and Rural Banks (Sixth District,
1966)

Deposit Size ($ Millions)	Percentage of Banks Using the Market	
	Urban	Rural
Less than 5	44.1%	21.3%
5 to 25	58.5	33.7
25 and over	96.7	68.2

Source: Survey questionnaire for Brandt and Crowe: internal files, Federal Reserve Bank of Atlanta, June, 1967. Urban banks are defined as those located in one of the District's 28 Standard
Metropolitan Statistical Areas.

Another relationship of significance in explaining the differences between Federal funds traders and non-traders is the urban-rural division; a
far greater proportion of urban banks trade Federal funds than do rural
banks of the same size (Table 3). This finding is in ready accord with
the intuitive feeling that urban banks have better access to money market
information and can more easily attract sophisticated management personnel.

The attitude of a bank's management toward borrowing money also has an
impact on the decision of whether to trade Federal funds. There is a con-
servative tradition among bankers under which the borrowing of money, a-
side from accepting funds from one's own depositors, is considered to be
an unsound financial practice.[1] Over time, political enlightenment and

---

1. See Chapter II, p. 53.

economic necessity have eroded this tradition, but its strength remains among small banks, particularly in rural areas and in the Southeast. Even the large money market banks prefer to reduce or eliminate their borrowing levels on call report dates, so that their published financial statements will portray what they consider to be a more favorable financial picture.

In 1966, for example, a year of record credit demands, the majority of the member banks in the Atlanta District did no borrowing of any kind. Thus to a great extent the question of whether to borrow Federal funds is part of the larger question of whether to borrow at all. And the evidence shows that only a very few of those banks which refuse to borrow funds are willing to lend their own reserves to others, an attitude which may be typified by the comment of one Louisiana banker. He remarked that he had stayed out of the market during 1966 in distrust of the financial condition of the New York banks which were doing most of the borrowing. It perhaps would be inconsistent for a banker to refuse to borrow and yet to be willing to lend funds to other banks; in this manner nearly three hundred banks in the Sixth District eliminated themselves from the market in 1966.

Several other characteristics of District banks were examined. It was thought that banks doing a relatively heavy traffic in correspondent banking would be more likely to be involved in the interbank loan market; that banks with high ratios of loans to deposits would be more likely to maintain a tight reserve position; that banks paying high rates on time deposits would be most aggressive in bidding for reserve funds as well; that banks with heavy investments in loans to business or to banks rather than to consumers or farmers would have a greater demand for a short-term adjustment mechanism; and that banks with high levels of volatile government deposits or general demand deposits would be more likely to make reserve adjustments through the funds market. None of these effects showed any significance in the data examined for this study. In summary, six factors were found to be conducive to a bank's participation in the Federal funds market:

1. large size
2. location in an economic area causing deposit volatility, such as a resort or a port city
3. location in an urban area
4. dwindling profit margins
5. a rapid growth rate
6. a positive attitude toward borrowing.

Flows of Federal Funds

The geographic pattern in which money flows through the Federal funds market has substantial social and economic implications. The funds market should serve to reallocate funds in favor of areas with relatively heavy credit demands. Idle balances are activated, and low-return assets can be dropped for more favorable investments. Therefore the pattern of geographic flows should indicate the regions of the country in which net excesses prevail in either the supply of or the demand for bank credit. The absence of universal data on these flows is unfortunate for this reason. The first comprehensive Federal Reserve survey was completed in 1959 and led to the conclusion that

> Banks in the New York District were the largest net buyers of Federal funds, their total purchases being more than double their total sales. Banks in the Chicago District purchased substantially more than they sold; the Atlanta and Dallas Districts also had net purchases, but too small to be significant. In the remainder of the districts, sales exceeded purchases. Thus, out of a network of transactions crisscrossing the United States, the net result appeared to be an inflow of Federal funds to New York City and, to a lesser extent, Chicago.[1]

Those conclusions were based on a sample of 150 of the most active trading banks, on data covering only one month, November, 1956. In order to improve on the reliability of the report, a three-year study was undertaken by the Federal Reserve System using a sample of 250 banks for the 1959-1962 period. Its main findings supported the preliminary work. New York City banks were found frequently to average net purchases in excess of $400 million per day, with about one fourth of that sum coming from banks elsewhere in the New York District. Other regions ran both net selling and net buying positions at various times during the period. The Chicago District had net purchases averaging about $100 million per day through 1960 and early 1961, then turned and sold similar net sums for the following year and a half. The San Francisco district, as before, was a net seller of funds most of the time.[2] Atlanta area banks were net buyers of about $30 million per day for the first nine months of the survey, but they sold funds regularly during the last two years, ending about even for the full period.

---

1. Board of Governors, The Federal Funds Market, p. 7.

2. Dorothy M. Nichols, Trading in Federal Funds (Washington: Board of Governors, 1965), pp. 71-79.

Conclusions

The purpose of this chapter has been to provide background material for a study of the effects of the Federal funds market on the transmission of monetary policy. Some general observations are of interest:

1. Regulatory and policy-making officials, including those of the Federal Reserve, have taken a highly favorable attitude toward the funds market. This favor is reflected in the various rulings from 1928 to 1964 which increased the ability of bankers to engage in interbank transfers of reserves. The legal base of the market is now firmly established.

2. The funds market has indeed increased the efficiency of the reserve base. Banks which trade funds actively are able to run lower balances of idle funds than they would if the market were not available to them. Even though the increased profitability of this operation did not show up in the limited data used in the third section of the chapter, it is nonetheless clear that the economic base of the market is very well established. It has yet to be determined whether this effect is as stable and predictable as the Federal Reserve believes it to be.

3. Some evidence has been produced to support the conclusion of Federal Reserve officials that "through this market the initial effects of Federal Reserve operations are more rapidly transmitted from the central money market to banks throughout the country."[1] When policy is tightened, the "central money market" banks may increase purchases of funds through the national market, spreading the effects of the policy change. When policy is eased these purchases can be reduced. However, this background material leaves unanswered the question of whether the act of altering flows into the money market itself significantly offsets the policy action; after all, net purchases do seem to move inversely to the policy change.

4. The extreme concentration of purchases in a few large banks reduces the dimensions of the analysis problem. Even though there may be as many as 3500 participants in the market at any one time, the magnitude of trading volume can be measured fairly accurately through the purchases of the few most active banks.

5. Price effects have been considered only in passing throughout this chapter. To policy officials, changes in prevailing interest rates charged for funds and the impacts of those changes on the general level of interest rates may be of the utmost importance. Those effects are the subject of the next chapter.

---

1. Ibid., p. 8.

Chapter Two. The Role of the Interest Rate

Introduction

The interest rate on Federal funds is determined by the prevailing conditions of demand and supply in the markets for bank reserves. These conditions in turn are a function of demands for bank credit, supplies of reserves from the Federal Reserve, and interest rates in closely related markets. In terms of price theory, Federal funds have a derived demand, owing its existence to general demands for credit. These reserve funds are used as a raw material in the production of bank deposits, a material with a number of nearly perfect substitutes. Their supply is determined by relative prices.

The plan of this chapter is to analyze each of the major factors affecting these demand and supply functions. This introductory section examines the general nature of the demand for borrowed reserves. Then the short-run "personality" of the interest rate is described as a function of changes in the supply of Federal Reserve credit. The remainder of the chapter is devoted to a discussion of the substitutability of Federal funds with the discount window and with transfers of secondary reserves, and the effects of these relationships on the interest rate.

In practice, rates are determined by the banks which are buying Federal funds. The large New York banks will make decisions continuously as to the volume of funds they need to attract in order to satisfy both their reserve position and their loan portfolio. If their own credit demands are rising, they may increase their offering rates on Federal funds in order to attract a greater volume of reserves through the market. These rates then are quoted to potential sellers around the country. They may be adjusted quickly, sometimes quite often, if they are out of line with the quotations of their competitors as far away as San Francisco, Chicago, or Dallas, or if they are drawing in a volume of funds different from the supply which was anticipated. Through the correspondent system this same set of rates filters through the market to the multitude of sellers in

each district. Ceteris paribus, an increase in demand for bank credit
will cause prices to rise in the Federal funds market.[1]

One major item in the ceteris suitcase is the supply of Federal Reserve
credit. A positive demand for Federal funds requires not only heavy demands for credit but also an inadequate supply of unborrowed reserves.
Each individual bank has its own portfolio requirements; normally these
requirements are set so as to maximize the earning potential of the bank's
assets, subject to liquidity and safety constraints imposed by management
decision and by regulatory authority.[2] These constraints take the form of
legal requirements for minimum holdings of primary reserves and of management requirements for minimum holdings of secondary reserves and excess
primary reserves. Still another constraint is that interest rates paid on
primary reserves are pegged permanently at zero. Prices of secondary reserves, other investments, and bank loans can be varied to equilibrate each
market. This elementary model of bank behavior illustrates the derived
nature of the demand for Federal funds. All the banker wants to do is to
acquire enough (non-earning) reserves to support the demands on his asset
portfolio at prevailing interest rates. If these reserve funds are available at no cost--that is, if the volume of unborrowed reserves supplied by
the Federal Reserve is adequate to meet the demands for reserves by the
aggregate system of banks--then there will be only some minimum demand for
borrowed reserves, which involve a positive cost. This minimum demand will
represent the amount of reserve redistribution made necessary by the difference between the distribution of Federal Reserve credit and the distribution of demands for commercial bank credit.

Suppose that the banking system has a positive aggregate demand for
excess reserves. The argument actually is unaffected by the sign of this
demand, but the assumption simplifies the exposition somewhat. The Federal

1. If the Federal funds rate initially is equal to the discount rate,
it may be possible for an increase in the demand for Federal funds not to
generate a price increase. This constraint is developed more fully below,
in this chapter and the next (pp. 44-48 and 62-64).

2. For a more complete discussion of bank portfolio models, see the
various papers in Kalman J. Cohen and Frederick S. Hammer, Analytical Methods in Banking (Homewood, Ill.: Richard D. Irwin, 1966). A broad outline
for the type of model presented here was suggested in James L. Pierce,
"Commercial Bank Liquidity," Federal Reserve Bulletin, LII (August, 1966),
1093-1101.

Reserve System, pursuant to the instructions of the Federal Open Market
Committee (FOMC), will supply at any given moment some level of unborrowed
reserves to the member banks, and this level will imply some positive or
negative level of unborrowed excess reserves, commonly known as free reserves. The precise objective of the FOMC policy is immaterial. The committee may attempt to hit a target level of free reserves or perhaps to
alter the level of long-term corporate bond rates. Regardless of the target being pursued, the use of unborrowed reserves as a policy instrument
will result in free reserves being partly a function of the policy decision.[1] Whenever this level of free reserves is below the system's demand
for excess reserves, there will arise a derived demand for borrowed reserves.

The most obvious way to satisfy this demand would be to borrow reserves
through the discount window, increasing the total volume of reserves to
the desired level. But this process may be limited by the Reserve officials, who can increase the cost of such borrowing either by raising the
discount rate charged or by increasing their non-price constraints on borrowing. The existence of these constraints, which might take the form of
selective sanctions or simply of refusals to extend credit to banks in particular situations, could make bankers less willing to use the window. If
for any of these reasons the cost of discounting becomes high relative to
other means of acquiring reserve funds, it will be abandoned in favor of
the more competitive instruments.

One method which may be competitive at times is that of selling secondary reserves. These are highly liquid assets which usually earn lower
returns than the bulk of a bank's portfolio but which can be converted
readily to primary reserves when necessary. It seems intuitively clear
that the portion of total assets to be held in secondary reserves would be
dependent partly on relative interest rates. If the earnings being sacri-
ficed are large, banks should be less willing to hold a cushion of "protective investments" than if the sacrifice were small.[2] Therefore, if bank

1. The true instrument being used is the power to buy and sell assets
for the system's open market account; unborrowed reserves are a "proximate
target" of changes in this account. For purposes of this discussion, that
refinement may be ignored. See Chapter V (p. 107) for a more complete
discussion of the point.

2. A. James Meigs presents a model of this type in his monograph, Free
Reserves and the Money Supply (Chicago: University of Chicago Press, 1962).
The term "protective investments" is from Roland I. Robinson, The Manage-
ment of Bank Funds (Second Edition; New York: McGraw-Hill, 1962), p. 14.

credit demands are sufficiently high, the banking system might be able to shift some part of its portfolio from secondary reserves into loans, permitting a given supply of primary reserves to support a larger volume of bank loans. As Warren Smith observed in the mid-1950's,[1] this phenomenon at times can be a very powerful force. In particular the selling of Treasury bills, by far the most widely used secondary reserve, may be a major source of reserves for credit expansion.

This conversion process does not change the volume of existing reserves. It does, however, increase what might be called the "loan velocity" of reserves, the ratio of loans to reserves. This velocity concept will be discussed in detail in the next chapter, but it serves as the basis for an understanding of the role of the interest rate as an equilibrating force in reserve markets. If bank portfolios contained only two items, reserves and earning assets, and if reserves were always a fixed portion of total assets, then the volume of earning assets would always be in a fixed proportion to the reserves supporting them. In fact, the legal reserve ratios set a maximum to this proportion, and the observed figures are always below it to the extent that banks are holding either excess or secondary reserves.

It is at this point that the Federal funds rate enters the picture. If an increase in the funds rate can be used to induce some banks to hold a smaller cushion of excess primary reserves than they otherwise would, then the total velocity of reserves can be increased. By legal constraint, banks earn no explicit return on these excesses, and they hold them only for liquidity in the face of uncertain reserve flows. An increase in the sacrifice imposed on such holdings should make banks less willing to hold them. When the funds rate is raised, reserves which had been idle, presumably at banks with relatively light credit demands, may be shifted to active accounts at banks with heavy credit demands, enabling these same reserves to support a greater volume of loans.

There are thus three major short-run adjustment mechanisms which can be used to combat reserve shortages: borrowing reserves through the discount window, selling secondary reserves, and buying primary reserves from other banks. The first of these directly increases the volume of total reserves. The second leaves this volume unchanged but increases the "loan velocity" of reserves. The third increases total reserve velocity.

---

1. "On the Effectiveness of Monetary Policy," American Economic Review, XLVI (September, 1956), 588-606.

Other methods exist, for banks always can attempt to create additional
deposits through advertising, increased interest rates or other benefits,
or increased compensating-balance requirements. They also can borrow money
on short-term promissory notes in some states, and they can raise additional capital.[1] One other method which is highly competitive with new
time deposits at major banks is the Euro-dollar market. Banks with foreign
branches can increase deposits at those branches rather than in domestic
offices, thereby avoiding interest rate ceilings.[2] But none of these methods are really competitive with the Federal funds market or the other
sources of immediate funds. They are generally costlier and are better
suited to long-run or continuing problems. As Fred H. Klopstock of the
Federal Reserve Bank of New York has written of the Euro-dollar market,
"banks seldom use Euro-dollar balances for specifically adjusting day-to-
day cash and reserve positions except over weekends. The Euro-dollar market is generally not suited to immediate reserve adjustment needs."[3] This
is not intended to underplay the importance of these markets but merely to
indicate that they are not primary substitutes for the markets in which we
are interested here. It is even possible that the Euro-dollar market
serves more as a complement than a substitute for Federal funds, since
foreign banks may acquire dollar balances for the specific purpose of reselling them in the United States funds market.[4] Unfortunately, there
seems to be no good data series on such activity.

The Personality of the Funds Rate

It may be inferred from the above discussion that the two closest substitutes for a purchase of Federal funds are borrowings at the discount
window and sales of secondary reserves, particularly Treasury bills. The

1. The recent spreading of one-bank holding companies has greatly in-
creased the scope of non-deposit sources of funds. See G. Dale Weight, "A
Note on Some Sources of Nondeposit Bank Funds," Federal Reserve Bank of
Cleveland Economic Commentary, (August 11, 1969).

2. Prior to September 4, 1969, banks also could avoid reserve requirements by such transfers. That loophole was closed by an amendment to
Regulation D.

3. "Euro-Dollars in the Liquidity and Reserve Management of United
States Banks," Federal Reserve Bank of New York Monthly Review, L (July,
1968), 133.

4. Ibid., p. 134.

effects of these relationships on the funds rate will be the subject of
the next section. Before proceeding to that topic, it may be useful to
examine the effects of changes in Federal Reserve credit. All of the other
forces mentioned above are fairly stable. The cost of borrowing at the
Federal Reserve has changed quite slowly over most of the post-Accord
period. Loan demand will vary quite a bit over the business cycle but
exhibits little short-term volatility. Bill rates do exhibit some wide
swings, but at least part of that is an effect from, rather than a cause
of, fluctuations in the funds rate. On the other hand, the supply of reserves undergoes very wide and sudden swings over short-run periods.
When these daily movements are averaged out, the reserve supply appears to
be rather stable. Consequently, the other forces may be more important in
the long-run determination of funds rates, but changes in Federal Reserve
credit are the largest single cause of the very short-run volatility which
this series exhibits.

The most common manifestation of this relationship is that the funds
rate will from time to time fall sharply below its normal pattern for one
or two days and then return. These drops can be several percentage points
in magnitude, completely eliminating the supply of funds into the market.
For examples of the way this process operates, consider the period of
tight monetary policy which began with the discount rate increase of November, 1964 and ran for about 100 weeks. During this time policies were
designed to push interest rates upward by providing for continuing reserve
shortages in the open market. However, on several occasions the supply of
reserves rose quite rapidly for brief periods, causing the funds rate to
fall. Figure 1 shows the differential between the funds rate and the bill
rate for each of those 100 weeks; about one of every ten weekly figures is
out of line with the normal pattern, almost always because of reserve
swings. The ten points which have been isolated are not only the lowest
points on the graph but also are substantially (at least forty basis
points) below the points on either side. An enumeration of the circumstances related to each of these points serves to illustrate the variety
of factors acting on the funds rate.

1. November 28, 1964. As is standard practice, the Federal Reserve
System supplied temporary surpluses in unborrowed reserves when it increased the discount rate, in order to effect adjustments gradually. The funds
rate accordingly fell to low levels for the first two days under the new

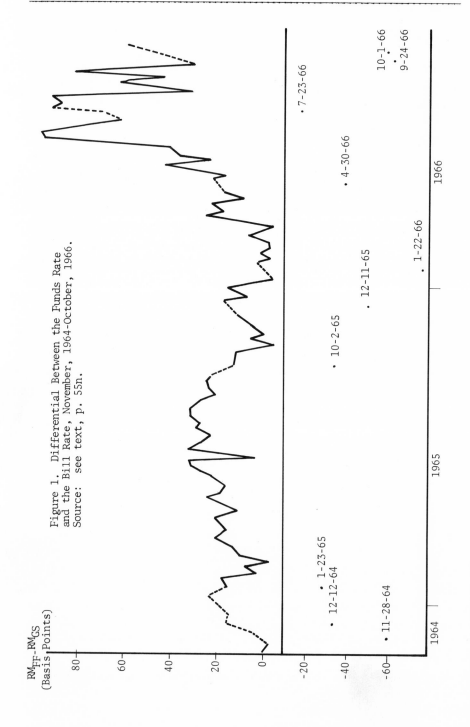

Figure 1. Differential Between the Funds Rate
and the Bill Rate, November, 1964-October, 1966.
Source: see text, p. 55n.

discount rate. During the week free reserves rose nearly $100 million
from previous levels near zero.

2. December 12, 1964. During the intervening two weeks several major
banks announced increases in their prime lending rates in response to the
discount rate hike. Citizens and Southern in Atlanta began the move on
November 27, First National of Boston followed four days later, and a band-
wagon appeared to be forming by December 2. That night President Johnson
made a speech warning banks not to raise their lending rates and advising
those which already had done so to rescind their actions. Within two days
almost all banks were back to their 4 1/2% prime rates. For several days
following this maneuver, demand for business loans tapered off because of
uncertainty as to future rates, and bank demand for reserves fell accordingly. But the Federal Reserve apparently failed to predict this decline,
and free reserves rose by nearly $250 million in two weeks. The funds rate
was depressed for a few days during this period.

3. January 23, 1965. Every year about one month after Christmas
there is a heavy inflow of cash to commercial banks and a temporary lull
in deposits. This usually causes free reserves to jump sharply for a few
days. In 1965, free reserves rose by $120 million, and the funds rate
fell by about 2 1/2 percentage points for two days.

4. October 2, 1965. A seemingly capricious increase in Federal Reserve float of about $700 million per day during the middle of September
caused reserves to pile up throughout the two-week computation period ending September 29. As a delayed reaction the attempts to sell these reserves at the last minute caused the funds rate to hit zero on the 29th.
The average rate for that day was 1%.

5. December 11, 1965. Another discount rate increase during the week
was accompanied by the same sort of temporary reserve injection described
for the 1964 increase. Free reserves rose by about $100 million.

6. January 22, 1966. The same seasonal pattern as prevailed a year
earlier brought a one-week increase in free reserves of almost $350 mil-
lion.

7. April 30, 1966. After the filing deadline for personal income
taxes, some $3.3 billion in government deposits poured into the banking
system. This inflow provided funds sufficient to meet loan demand, reducing demand for Federal funds temporarily.

8. July 23, 1966. The nation's worst airline strike in history prevented the normal clearing of checks, causing unpredictable swings in

Federal Reserve float. On several occasions during the early days of the
strike, the funds market softened considerably.

9 and 10. September 24 and October 1, 1966. At the climax of the
1966 credit crunch, Congress had passed a bill granting new discretionary
powers to the Federal Reserve and other agencies to regulate maximum interest rates on particular classes and maturities of deposits and other
instruments.[1] On September 21, these powers were signed into law by President Johnson; numerous adjustments in the ceiling rates were put into effect
immediately by the agencies. Again, to aid banks in adjusting to the new
rates, the Federal Reserve temporarily increased reserve supplies, depress-
ing the funds market for two or three weeks.

The types of volatility described above appear periodically, and the
reserve authorities have the capability to offset each of them and to provide for a smooth pattern in short-term rates. Perhaps the truly distin-
guishing feature of the examples given is that the magnitudes seem to have
been forecast incorrectly by the Federal Reserve, so that its defensive
open market operations failed to offset them. For example, it would seem
reasonable to expect the Federal Reserve, when it raises the discount rate,
to offset the effects of the increase by no more than the magnitude of
those effects. However, in both cases above, the weeks in which the rate
was increased were characterized by sharply easier conditions in the reserve markets. At the same time, the impacts of the various circumstances
may have been incorrectly forecast by the bankers in the market. In most
cases, the actual increases in reserves occurred several days before they
found their way into increased supplies in the funds market. Reserve increases early in a two-week computation period were permitted to build
into large excesses before the banks all tried to sell them in a saturated
market on the last day or two of the period. During the week ending September 22, 1965 (point 4 above) there was a $700 million increase in float
which was completely wiped out in the following week; yet there was no
weakening of the funds rate until the final day of that reserve period,
September 29. In fact, the effective rate hit what was then a record high
of 4 1/4% on the 23rd before falling to 1% six days later. For all of
these reasons the presence of large and unpredictable swings in the components of Federal Reserve credit has been a cause of considerable short-
term volatility in the interest rate on Federal funds.

---

1. Federal Reserve Act, 12 CFR 371b, as amended September 21, 1966.

These last few paragraphs have demonstrated another characteristic of Federal funds with an important bearing on the interest rate: purchases and sales of Federal funds are nearly perfect substitutes for transfers on other days of the same reserve period but have almost zero substitutability with transactions on dates outside of the period. Bank reserves are storable at low cost for a few days and become totally valueless at the end of each period. Consider a bank with accumulated excess reserves of $1 million five days before the end of its computation period. The bank can sell these funds on any one of the five remaining days; the effect on its reserve position will be the same. If a bank expects to gain $1 million in reserves on the last day of the period, it can sell the money for one day now or wait until it has the funds in hand; the timing again is immaterial. But if the bank still has an excess at the end of the period, it cannot carry it over to the next term, and the funds become worthless. Similarly, a bank with a reserve shortage or an expected shortage can borrow money at any time during the period but is fairly strictly limited by the computation dates.

Several exceptions need to be noted. First, a bank cannot sell on any day a larger amount than it currently has in its account with the Federal Reserve. This qualification is not as trivial as it at first seems. Suppose our bank has an average reserve requirement of $10 million and has just run an average balance of $13 million for the first six days of its computation week. On the last day we have an accumulated excess of $18 million, but we are able to sell only $13 million with a resulting opportunity cost of perhaps $750 in lost interest receipts (if the rate is about 5%). This factor limits the substitutability of sales on different days of the period by making early sales more desirable.

Second, since September, 1968 banks have been able to carry over a reserve excess or deficit so long as it does not exceed 2% of the average requirement and as long as it is offset within the next period.[1] This change increases the substitutability of transfers on different days by reducing the cost of guessing wrong at the end of the period. Its quantitative importance obviously is quite limited.

The third point probably is the most significant. Banks face stochastic reserve flows throughout each period, and as they approach the final

1. Board of Governors, _Regulation D_, as amended September 12, 1968.

day the opportunities for reacting to unexpected shocks become steadily reduced. This increases the relative value of early purchases; if a bank
runs a deficit early in the period, later on it may find itself with ab-
normally large deficiencies which are difficult and costly to erase. More
importantly, however, the relative desirability of delayed sales is increased. By the end of the period the bank has an improved view of its
average reserve position and can sell its excesses with confidence. Pre-
mature sales may necessitate purchases later on which should result in the
funds rate falling toward the end of the computation week.

Fourth, there is the possibility that expectations of changes in interest rates during the reserve period will lead banks to alter the timing of
their transfers. One manifestation of this effect would be delaying of
sales as long as possible when rates are rising, and similar speculative
moves in other circumstances. Another expression would be selling short
in order to take advantage of anticipated rate weaknesses at the end of
the period. Some bankers will perceive a lower-than-average risk pattern,
either because their reserve position is relatively stable or because
their nerves are relatively strong. They can profit by selling funds regularly on Thursdays and Fridays and buying them back on the following Tues-
day or Wednesday when the rates should be depressed because of the sorts
of uncertainty described above.

If this arbitrage mechanism were very powerful, the "Wednesday weakness" could be almost completely eliminated. On the other hand, the uncertainty which is inherent in the process of reserve calculation has to
reduce somewhat the substitutability of funds transfers at different points
in time. If the banker faced complete certainty as to his reserve position
over the current reserve period, he would be indifferent to the timing of
his purchases or sales as long as he could prevent his accumulated excess
from exceeding his present reserve balance. As uncertainty rises, he increasingly will favor surpluses (or smaller deficits) early in the period
by accelerating his purchases and delaying his sales. Consequently, in all
real circumstances, the interest rate on transfers of funds should be lower
on average at the end of the period than in the opening days. The opportunity to gain from interest arbitrage always exists, but it should be limited by the costs associated with the first three points listed above (pp.
39-40).

Two more factors need to be mentioned before an empirical test of this
hypothesis can be presented. Loans of Federal funds, by definition, carry

a maturity of one business day. Loans made on Friday bring in three days'
interest for the same transfer cost as a one-day loan, and purchases made
on Friday bring in three days of reserve balances for the same cost. The
result is that weekend transfers are more desirable than those made Monday
through Thursday. However, if the magnitude of this effect is similar on
both sides of the market, there should be no effect on the interest rate.

Finally, there is the dichotomy between city and country banks. Prior
to September, 1968, country banks were permitted to average their reserve
balances over a two-week period, while city banks were given only a one-
week leeway. Because the city banks are net buyers of funds and the country banks net sellers, the greatest weakness in the funds rate should have
come at the end of the two-week period when both classes reckoned their
positions. On the odd weeks, there was no particular reason to expect demand not to hold up solidly.

Taken together, these several factors should result in the Federal
funds rate being highest on Thursday and Fridays (the opening days of the
reserve periods), only slightly softer from Monday to Wednesday of the odd
weeks, but at its lowest on those days of even weeks when all reserve periods are coming to a close. If complete interest arbitrage is occurring,
these remaining differentials should reflect the subjective costs which
banks associate with the factors listed above.

Figure 2 summarizes the data on these relationships over two periods
of time, each exactly four years in length. During the first period, ending in October, 1964, the discount rate was serving as an effective ceiling on movements in the funds rate. In the second period, the funds rate
was able to move freely with no effective upward boundary. The chart presents, for each time period, the mean level of the Federal funds rate, net
of the discount rate, for each day of the average reserve computation period. During the first four years shown, the funds rate averaged about
thirty basis points below the discount rate on each of the first six days
of the computation period, weakening slightly on the seventh and eighth
business days and plunging sharply at the end of the second week. The same
type of pattern prevailed during the next four years except at higher
levels. It is interesting to note that there seems to be no tendency over
time to reduce the weakness displayed on even Tuesdays and Wednesdays; one
could conclude from this either that the market still is failing to arbitrage existing rate differentials, or--more likely--that these differentials

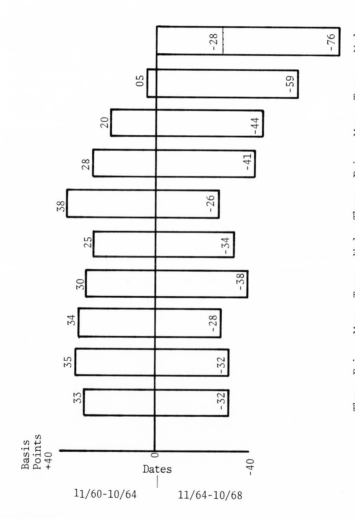

Figure 2. Differential Between the Funds Rate and the Discount Rate, Averaged by Days of the Reserve Computation Period, 1960-1968. Source: see text, p. 55n.

represent a risk premium as the day of reckoning approaches. The latter possibility is discussed at length in Chapter IV (pp. 93-96).

Actually the use of means for this purpose is a bit misleading, since the data are not distributed normally around the figures shown. What in fact is observed is that the funds rate either holds firm at the end of the period, or else it falls to very low levels; this bimodal distribution, with a range that increases markedly toward the end of the biweekly period, produces the declining means shown in the chart. Here it is sufficient to note that the general tendencies hypothesized about intraweekly rate movements are verified by the data.

Suppose for the moment that all of the differences between rates early in the period and rates at the end of the period can be attributed to a rational assessment of the costs of uncertainty. A somewhat arbitrary evaluation of these costs can then be made as follows. Take the average of the last two daily rates in each period (those on even Tuesdays and Wednesdays) as representative of the rates prevailing under pressure from the sudden release of pent-up supplies of funds. Take the highest two rates in the period as representative of normal supply conditions. If the averaging of two rates is sufficient to reduce the importance of extreme conditions (and an examination of daily figures indicates that this should be true), then the difference between the average high rates and the average ending rates should be a fairly reliable measure of the costs of uncertainty as seen by the bankers in the market. The mean value of this figure over the eight-year period was 56 basis points. For each of the four-year subperiods, it was again 56 points. One may conclude that the market does not view transfers of Federal funds on different days within a computation period as perfectly substitutable goods.

One final note before leaving this topic. The recent amendments to Regulation D eliminated the biweekly computation period, putting all banks on the same timetable. Data for the first year of the new scheme suggest that the degree of uncertainty in the funds market has not been reduced sufficiently to affect the rate pattern:

Day of period	Average excess of funds rate over discount rate
Thursday	179 basis points
Friday	186
Monday	166
Tuesday	124
Wednesday	74

The Funds Rate and the Discount Window

For a bank with a temporary reserve shortage, the two least costly
solutions under most circumstances are the discount window and the Federal
funds market. The effect on the individual bank's balance sheet is identical, regardless of which source is used. The two are perfect substitutes
from that view, so that we can treat them as having one composite demand
curve, the demand for borrowed reserves. Each good, however, has a separate supply function. Consider first the discount window. The discount
rate is pegged by the Federal Reserve and normally is changed infrequently,
lagging behind other short-term interest rates. But the discount rate is
not the full cost of borrowing from the Reserve Bank. Each member bank is
expected to limit its total borrowing and to repay any loans quickly. Extended borrowing may result in the imposition of sanctions against the bank
in the form of closer examinations, reduction or suspension of borrowing
privileges, or other types of worsened relations between the bank and the
Fed.[1] The supply curve seen by the bank may be horizontal at the discount
rate over some range of borrowing, but it certainly will slope upward after
some point and eventually will become vertical at the maximum borrowing
level permitted by the discount officials. The supply curve for the market will have the same shape, being a horizontal summation of the supplies
extended to individual banks. Note that Reserve officials can and do practice discrimination by isolating each bank and using non-price rationing.
The resale market is watched closely; banks found to be reselling reserves
borrowed from the Fed are reprimanded. The only difference between this
and the classical case of price discrimination is that the justification
is not that demand elasticities differ among buyers, but rather that the
supply elasticities are established separately by policy decisions based
on the circumstances of the individual case. The goal is not to maximize
revenue but to distribute reserves in a way deemed optimal by policy officials.

The supply curve for Federal funds, as seen by a single bank, will have
a shape similar to the supply curve from the discount window. It will be
horizontal over some initial range. The bank, which may be a pure competi-

---

1. For an inside view of this process, see Clay J. Anderson, Evolution of the Role and Functioning of the Discount Mechanism (Washington:
Board of Governors, 1966).

tor or an oligopsonist in this market, cannot attract any funds by offering a rate lower than the rate established by the rest of the market. But it may be able to increase the supply beyond what it is able to draw at the market rate by offering a slightly higher price. Its supply curve there-fore will have a positive slope over some range. But if it offers a price very much higher than the market rate, lenders will become increasingly suspicious of the quality of these loans. After all, the sums of money involved in this game are enormous; lending banks rightfully are hesitant to extend credit to banks whose balance sheets are unusually illiquid, and the offering of steadily increasing rates to attract funds may be taken as a sign of such a weakness. Each bank will have some level of borrowing at which the supply function which it faces becomes vertical.

The market supply curve will be more positively sloped than that of the individual seller, in classical competitive fashion. There will be a mini-mum interest rate, representing transfer costs, at which no funds will be forthcoming. As the rate increases, ever greater supplies will result. The process will stop at some maximum level, but since additional supplies can be generated by selling investments or even loans, this maximum should not be an effective constraint.

Figure 3 illustrates these relationships. The supply curves for reserves from the discount window and borrowed Federal funds are summed to yield a market supply of borrowed reserves. This supply, of course, will not be equal to the Federal Reserve figure for borrowed reserves, but will instead be equal to that figure plus the purchases of Federal funds by all banks. Even though these open market purchases do not increase total re-serves, they may, at least in part, increase the sum of active reserve bal-ances.

An important byproduct of this analysis is that the true cost of bor-rowing reserve funds is no longer ambiguous. The total cost of borrowing from the Federal Reserve is equal to the discount rate plus whatever cost is imposed through subjective sanctions. This total cost must be equal in equilibrium to the cost of borrowing in the funds market. Therefore, when-ever the funds rate is above the discount rate, the difference between them should be a very good indicator of the degree of non-price rationing being used at the discount window. In the diagram "cost" is simply the Federal funds rate.

Figure 3 still is not an altogether satisfactory representation of the market. It does not adequately bring out the time dimensions of the prob-

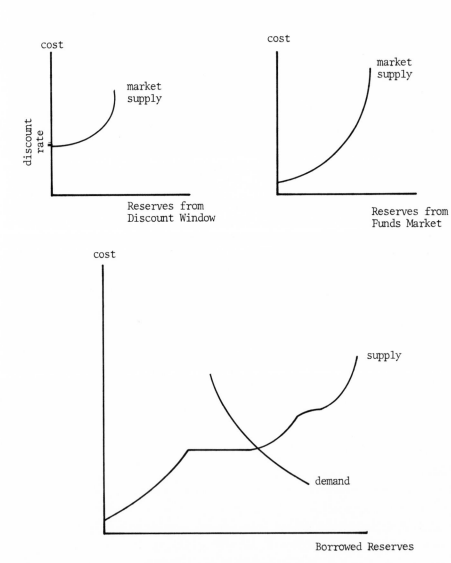

Figure 3. Equilibrium in the
Markets for Borrowed Reserves

lem, particularly as they relate to the discount window. The reference
for the flow of borrowed reserves must be some length of time; banks which
borrow continuously will meet with greater resistance than banks which borrow the same aggregate sum but with less regularity.[1] This result follows
from the Federal Reserve view that the window is appropriately used only
to cover temporary problems and not to provide a pool of lendable funds.
Another problem is that the aggregation over a system of banks obscures
distributional effects. The exact elasticities prevailing at any time will
depend not only on aggregate discount policy but also on the composition
of the banks which are using the window. Assume some initial collection
of borrowers; if one bank which has been borrowing for a long period drops
out and is replaced by another of the same size and with the same volume
of borrowing demands but which has not used the window recently, the market
supply function will shift to the right. Having noted this, one has only
to keep in mind that a fixed time dimension and borrower composition are
implicit in the construction of the curves.

The aggregate supply curve, shown in the bottom graph, has a prominent
shoulder at the discount rate, drawn on the assumption that reserves are
supplied freely through the discount window over some finite range. If
the total demand for borrowed reserves is low enough, the interest rate on
Federal funds will be below the discount rate, and all desired funds will
be obtained in the open market rather than through the window. The only
lending done by the Federal Reserve would be to those banks which, for one
or more of the reasons examined in the previous chapter (pp. 21-27), choose
not to avail themselves of the facilities of the funds market. As demand
rises, the supply and demand curves will intersect at the level of the discount rate over some finite domain. The funds rate will then equal the
discount rate, and many banks will be using both the discount window and
the funds market as sources of reserves. If demand continues to rise, the
cost of discounting will begin to include the non-price surveillance effects, and banks will prefer to pay premium rates in the interbank market
rather than beg at the central bank. During periods of extremely high demand the funds rate may rise considerably above the discount rate shoulder.

---

1. For a good exposition of the temporal dimensions of member-bank
borrowing, see Stephen M. Goldfeld and Edward J. Kane, "The Determinants
of Member-Bank Borrowing: an Econometric Study," Journal of Finance, XXI
(September, 1966), 505-509.

The Federal Reserve can influence this situation in several ways.
First, it can control demand through open-market policy. If an adequate
volume of unborrowed reserves is supplied, there will be little or no demand for borrowed reserves, as explained earlier (p. 31). Probably
the most important factor determining the level of demand is the current
status of open-market policy. Second, the discount rate may be changed,
displacing the kink in the supply curve. Third, policies of discount administration may be changed, altering the elasticity of the supply curve
to the right of the kink. The effect in any case will be to change both
the equilibrium level of borrowing and the prevailing interest rate in the
Federal funds market. The member banks can react to these policy changes
by altering the flow of funds through each market, but only by changing
the Federal funds rate. In order to offset a tightening of policy by increasing the flow of Federal funds, it is clear that the funds rate must be
increased.

Federal Funds, Treasury Bills, and
an Inventory Cycle

The unique feature of the relationship between purchases of Federal
funds and borrowings from the Federal Reserve is that each instrument has
the same effect on the borrower's balance sheet. An asset is created in
the form of a reserve balance. This asset is indistinguishable from reserves created in any other way. To the banker there is no such entry as
"borrowed reserves" or "free reserves" or any other division of total reserve balances. However, the various processes of reserve creation are
distinguished by the types of liabilities which are created. In the case
of the discount window the borrower incurs a debt to the Federal Reserve,
increasing its liability account entitled "rediscounts and other liabilities for borrowed money." If the reserves are acquired through the Federal funds market, a similar liability is created. Until recently funds purchases were reported to the Federal Reserve in that same "rediscounts and
other liabilities" figure. Starting with the call report of September,
1963 for national banks and December, 1965 for state-chartered member
banks, they have been listed separately as "Federal funds purchased."
Regardless of the form, the effect on the balance sheet is the same.

There are other sources from which banks may borrow, and they always
can try to attract additional deposit money as well. As was explained

earlier these methods generally are too costly to be used for short-term
purposes and are not really competitive in the same markets. But one method which is designed to remedy reserve pressures is the selling of secondary reserves. By definition these assets are held because they can readily
be converted to cash. The conversion process work differently from the
borrowing operation, because it merely substitutes one asset account for
another. This brings out the next important characteristic of Federal
funds: loans of Federal funds may be considered as secondary reserves to
the lender. Excess holdings of primary reserves are paid in exchange for
an asset which pays some interest but is readily convertible back into
cash. Such loans are very good substitutes for such other secondary reserves as Treasury bills,. other short-term government obligations, commercial paper, acceptances, and call loans. No bank, for example, would have
any reason to hold short-term commercial paper earning 4% interest if it
could sell that paper and then sell the proceeds as Federal funds earning
4 1/2%.

For comparative purposes it will be useful to let Treasury bills serve
as a proxy for all secondary reserves other than Federal funds. Bills not
only make up by far the largest portion of such assets; they also have the
most freely-moving and therefore the most representative interest rate.
Treasury bills also serve a unique function in bank portfolios, because
they are required collateral for Treasury Tax and Loan accounts, for most
loans obtained from the discount window, and for many loans through the
Federal funds market. These factors make Treasury bills uniquely suited
for comparison with holdings of loan paper from Federal funds sales.
Within some limited range, sales of Treasury bills may be substituted
freely for purchases of Federal funds. In a less limited way, purchases
of bills may be substituted for sales of funds.

A bank with excess reserves which are not expected to persist more
than a few days typically will be in the market for a secondary reserve.
In this context the Federal funds rate should be competitive with the
Treasury bill rate. Bankers may be expected to prefer to acquire which-
ever asset will provide the greater return, since each provides a similar
degree of safety and liquidity. A bank with a reserve shortage may or may
not be in the market selling secondary reserves; its first choice for a
solution to very temporary shortages probably will be borrowed money.
Furthermore, such a bank would not be likely to have any "Federal funds

sold" in its secondary reserve portfolio, so that the selling of that
asset (i.e., the non-renewal of the loan) is not likely to be a viable
alternative to selling one's Treasury bills. That is, for banks with reserve excesses, the choice between Federal funds and Treasury bills is one
of which secondary reserve to acquire. For banks with reserve shortages
the choice is whether to sell a secondary reserve (bills) or to borrow
money (Federal funds). Given this background, we can now speculate as to
the expected relationship between the interest rates on the two instruments.

It has been established above (see Figure 3, p. 46) that the Federal
funds rate will be determined by conditions of demand and supply in the
markets for borrowed reserves. What is proposed now is to add to the contents of those functions. Take Federal Reserve policy as given for the
moment, so that banks have a fixed volume of unborrowed reserves available
to them, and take the demand for credit to be fixed as well; then the demand for borrowed reserves may be considered to be a function of borrowing
costs relative to the costs of selling secondary reserves. The supply
curve for Federal funds will shift with changes in the relative yields
between funds and Treasury bills. For any given funds rate a higher yield
on bills will imply a lower supply of Federal funds, and conversely. Banks
with reserve excesses will have a greater preference for investing in
Treasury bills rather than in loans of reserves. These effects are shown
in Figure 4.

An increase in the Treasury bill rate should be accompanied by an increase in the Federal funds rate, unless the current equilibrium is on the
shoulder of the supply function and the shift is not so great as to move
the market onto a sloped section. Whenever the funds rate is equal to the
discount rate, small changes in the bill rate are not likely to disturb
that situation. Continued increases surely will cause the funds rate to
rise. Whether the change in total volume of borrowings rises or falls will
depend on the relative magnitudes of the demand and supply elasticities.

Now the assumption of fixed Federal Reserve policy may be relaxed. At
the same time, the assumption of fixed credit demands must be removed,
because one cannot speak of monetary policy except with regard to some set
of credit demands. If the latter increases and the same quantitative policies are maintained, the effect is the same as if the policies had been
tightened while demands for credit remained stable. In order to simplify
the discussion, active and passive restraints both will be considered to

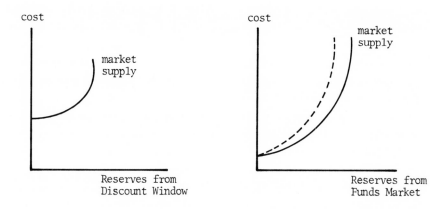

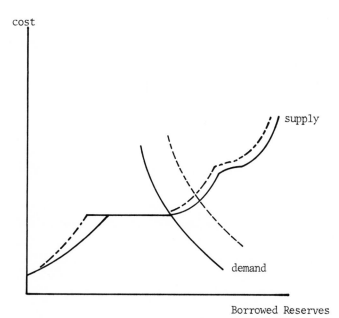

Figure 4. Effects of an Increase in the Bill
Rate on the Markets for Borrowed Reserves

be changes in policy. The primary effect of such changes on the market
for borrowed reserves will be a shift in the demand curve, since demand
has been shown to be derived from imbalances between credit demands and the
supply of unborrowed reserves. The supply curve also will shift; a tightening of policy will constrict the flow of Federal funds into the market.

Whether or not the shift in the demand curve results in a change in
the funds rate, it may nonetheless cause the bill rate to change. If we
start out on the shoulder of the supply curve for borrowed reserves and a
reduction in the supply of unborrowed reserves relative to credit demands
causes the demand curve to shift to the right along that shoulder, then
there will be no increase in the funds rate but there will be an increase
in discounting. At this point a new argument must be introduced. If
bankers are undisturbed by the increase in their indebtedness to the Reserve Bank (so long as the increase is not so great as to bring them into
the inelastic portion of the supply curve), then there will be no reason
to expect the Treasury bill rate or any other interest rate to rise under
the described circumstances. On the other hand, if bankers do exhibit a
reluctance to borrow, then any such increase in their indebtedness will
make the selling of secondary reserves relatively more attractive. This
selling pressure will push up the interest rate on Treasury bills.

To whatever strength is provided by the costs of reluctance may be
added the costs of rising supply curves once borrowing levels rise above
the shoulder. Whenever the funds rate increases, pressure must build up
on the bill rate. But if relative prices were the only important consideration, there would never be any reason to expect the two interest rates
to differ by very much; one would at least expect to find a fairly constant relationship between them. Such is not the case. From 1959 through
1969 the funds rate averaged just five basis points above the bill rate.
As might have been expected, the two prices will, in the long run, be
virtually equal.[1] But over shorter periods considerable differences may
be obtained. During one week in August, 1960 the average funds rate was
1.26 percentage points above the bill rate. One-half year later, it was
1.65 points below it for a week. During 1970 the funds rate averaged more
than a percentage point above the bill rate for six months; by early 1971

----

1. The mean difference of five basis points may be attributable to
the unique attractions of Treasury bills described above (p. 49).

the bill rate was once again the higher of the two. Clearly there is some force other than relative prices at work. That force may be the pressure of portfolio imbalance.

Two concepts mentioned in the course of this section may now be brought together: desired levels of secondary reserves and reluctance to borrow. Although the strength of the reluctance effect has been challenged on grounds that it violates the tenets of profit maximization,[1] its existence is well established in the academic literature, as is that of the protective-investment effect. The classic Chambers-Charnes model of portfolio management,[2] for example, assumes that banks desire to maximize profits subject to two constraints: that reserve requirements be met and that a "balanced portfolio" be maintained, the latter including minimum holdings of secondary reserves and other "minimum risk assets." The operational validity of these constraints is enhanced by the fact they were derived by Chambers and Charnes from the observed standards of bank examiners. Similar examples could be given readily. As for reluctance to borrow, Thomas Mayer in his recent book on monetary policy observes that "banks have a tradition against borrowing, a tradition at least in part explained by the disastrous effects of borrowing which showed up in nineteenth-century financial panics."[3]

If both of these forces are at work, then the recurring differences between funds rates and bill rates may be explained by the problems associated with attempts to maintain a portfolio which satisfies simultaneously the constraints on secondary reserves and on liabilities for borrowed money. Suppose that a bank is initially at a point of contrained optimization and is disturbed from that position by a tightening of monetary

---

1. See, for example, Anderson, pp. 14-22.

2. D. Chambers and A. Charnes, "Intertemporal Analysis and Optimization of Bank Portfolios," in Cohen and Hammer, pp. 67-86.

3. Monetary Policy in the United States (New York: Random House, 1968), p. 32. For statistical evidence in support of this contention, see the following articles by Murray Polakoff: "Reluctance Elasticity, Least Cost, and Member-Bank Borrowing: A Suggested Integration," Journal of Finance, XV (March, 1960), 1-18; "Federal Reserve Discount Policy and Its Critics," Banking and Monetary Studies, Deane Carson (ed.), (Homewood, Ill.: Richard D. Irwin, 1963), pp. 190-212; and (with William L. Silber) "Reluctance and Member-Bank Borrowing: Additional Evidence," Journal of Finance, XXII (March, 1967), 88-92. Also see Boughton, "The Effect of an Active Market in Federal Funds on the Transmission of Monetary Policy," Table 7, p. 54.

policy. In order to maintain its holdings of secondary reserves, the
initial response of the bank may be to borrow money from some source, perhaps the Federal funds market. If the tightening persists, the bank will
become increasingly reluctant to continue borrowing and will become more
and more willing to reduce its cushion of secondary reserves. That is,
the optimal level of protective investments, being partly a function of
the pressures on other parts of the balance sheet, will begin to fall.
The selling of Treasury bills gradually will replace the borrowing of reserves as the principal source of reserve funds. When the bank's holdings
of government securities have been depleted enough to fall below the optimum level corresponding to the bank's existing borrowing volume, then new
borrowing will be in order.

A similar response pattern will be generated by the easing of policy.
The initial response will be to repay borrowings and to refrain from additional borrowings. Once this has been accomplished, the bank's holdings
of secondary reserves may be replenished. If the easing of policy persists, however, the system will begin to build up bill holdings beyond desired levels and will attempt to increase sales of Federal funds. In the
face of general reserve availability there is likely to be insufficient demand for funds, and the interest rate will be driven downward. Although
it is not so likely in this case as in the case of tightening that pressures will be generated which are strong enough to produce a cyclical pattern in the interest rate, the potential at least is there for a fairly
minor cycle.

If this little story is a valid representation of bank response to
changes in Federal Reserve policy, then one would expect to find a continuing cyclical movement in the difference between the Federal funds rate
and the Treasury bill rate coinciding with the phases of a cycle in the
difference between actual and desired levels of Treasury bills, sold Federal funds, and liabilities for borrowed money. The latter cycle would be
very difficult to measure because of the need to acquire data which separate banks by principal buyers and principal sellers of funds and because of
the absence of a good measure of desired levels. Data are readily available for bill holdings of 341 weekly reporting banks, although the time
series contains several major breaks, reflecting changes in the composition
of the reporters. Data on Federal funds are available only for 46 large
banks. However, excellent data on interest rates are available and have
been compiled for this study over a period of almost 500 weeks beginning

in September, 1959.[1] A monthly series on the difference between the two rates is presented in Figure 5.

The average value of this difference, as mentioned above, is about five basis points. There is little or no trend in the series, but there is a clear cyclical pattern. The steep climb in the early months of the period coincides with the latter stages of the application of stringent monetary policy. This is followed by an equally steep descent as the minor recession of 1960-61 brought a turnabout in policy to active easing. Then the series calms down for several years; the cycle remains, but its amplitude is greatly reduced. The main policy action during this time was one of accommodation, of meeting most credit demands but keeping a grip on the handbrake. In late 1964 a sudden move toward tighter policies occurred, and the rate differential behaved like a cracked whip, generating ever-increasing amplitudes. The active easing of 1967 and 1968 caused wide gyrations in both rates; as expected, the two rates moved at different times, generating the observed oscillation.

The properties of the cycle in this series are not readily apparent from visual inspection of Figure 5. The irregularities, due at least in part to the constant application of varying doses of open-market policies, are too overwhelming. In order to test for the existence of a stable cycle in the rate differential and to determine its average periodicity, the statistical technique of spectral analysis may be employed. The object of spectral analysis is to decompose the variance of a stationary data series so that the portion of that variance associated with cycles of various frequencies is isolated.[2] The original data are transformed into

---

1. The daily data, from which weekly averages of Federal funds rates were calculated, are the effective rates computed by the Federal Reserve Bank of New York, Mabon Co., and Garvin Bantel Corp.; these effective rates are averages weighted by the volume of transactions occurring at different rates on each day. Weekly average Treasury bill rates were taken from the Federal Reserve Bulletin. Note that the weekly Federal funds rates published in the Bulletin are not suitable for statistical comparison because they are averaged over the reserve period (ending on Wednesday), while bill rates are averaged on the week ending Saturday. The latter standard is used here for both series.

2. For a description of this technique, see C.W.J. Granger and M. Hatanaka, Spectral Analysis of Economic Time Series (Princeton: Princeton University Press, 1964). The following discussion relies heavily both on that work and on Thomas H. Naylor, Kenneth Wertz, and Thomas H. Wonnacott, "Spectral Analysis of Data Generated by Simulation Experiments with Econometric Models," Econometrica, XXXVII (April, 1969), 333-352.

Figure 5. Differential Between the Funds
Rate and the Bill Rate, 1959-1969.
Source: monthly data, Federal Reserve Bulletin.

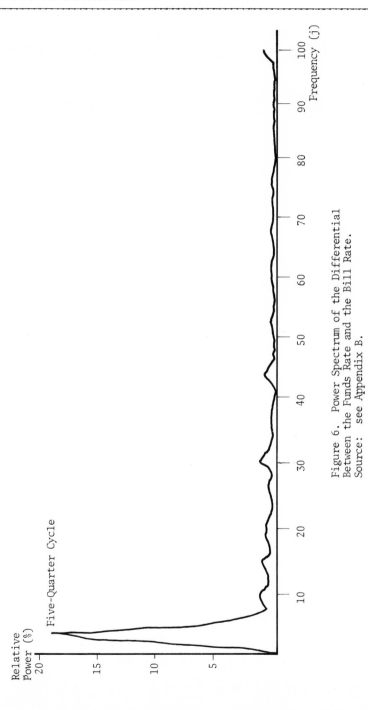

Figure 6. Power Spectrum of the Differential
Between the Funds Rate and the Bill Rate.
Source: see Appendix B.

the "frequency domain" through the estimation of a "power spectrum," the elements of which are the relative amplitudes of the various cycles. If the series does not exhibit a significant cyclical pattern, then a flat "white noise" pattern will appear. Spectral analysis may be compared with regression analysis: the latter decomposes the variance of a data series into elements which are associated with the contributions of each of several independent variables over the same time span, while the spectral technique decomposes the variance into elements associated with values of the original data series occurring at fixed intervals in the past. These elements of the variance may be interpreted as relative amplitudes, and the time lag associated with those amplitudes may be converted into the periods of the cycles generating the data stream. The present data series, as explained above, contains some 496 weekly observations, an adequate number for purposes of estimating the power spectrum of the differential.[1]

The most delicate problem in the spectral operation is determining the maximum cyclical period to estimate. Obviously cycles of great length cannot be estimated because of the lack of an adequate number of observations. The larger the number of cycles or "frequency bands" to be estimated, the lesser will be our ability to estimate the contribution of each band. It therefore is desirable to minimize the maximum lag or the maximum cycle length. On the other hand this minimization reduces the amount of information which can be obtained from the spectrum, particularly if we are interested in discovering the existence of rather long cycles. Visual inspection of Figure 5 indicates that the dominant cycle of the rate differential may be as long as a year and a half. To translate that period into the frequency domain, some new terminology is needed. Let

    n = the number of data observations,

    m = the number of frequency components or periods to be estimated,

    k = the period of a particular cycle, and

    j = the number of the frequency component associated with the cycle
        of period k.

That is, m components are estimated. The jth component will represent the relative amplitude of the cycle of period k, where k is computed by the formula $k = 2m/j$.[2] As an example, if we would like to inspect the contribution of a 1 1/2 year cycle, we could arbitrarily let m - 117 points;

---

1. Granger and Hatanaka (p. 61) observe that 200 observations "can be thought of as a desirable minimum" for estimating power spectra.

2. Naylor, Wertz, and Wonnacott, p. 341.

then the amplitude of the power spectrum at the third component (j = 3) would indicate the contribution of that cycle (k = 78 weeks).[1]

Granger and Hatanaka (p. 61) have speculated that a "reasonable" value for m would be in the range from n/5 to n/6. Since in the present case n = 496, this rule of thumb would suggest that from 80 to 100 components should be estimated. The final choice might be determined so as to "center" the observed cycles as well as possible; i.e., so that each relevant value of k will be a best estimate of the true period of the cycle. To illustrate this problem, let us suppose that the true generating cycle has a period of 78 weeks. We estimate the power spectrum of the sample data, using m = 90, and we discover a prominent peak at j = 2. This implies a value of k equal to 90 weeks. However, if m = 80, then an estimate of 80 weeks will be obtained for the period of the cycle. In most cases a little experimentation should reveal the best value to use for m. For the present study 100 frequency components were estimated.

The power spectrum of the rate differential is diagrammed in Figure 6. Its terrain is rather striking; aside from some minor undulations representing short cycles, there is only one prominent feature, located at the third frequency component. This location corresponds to a cycle with a period of approximately five calendar quarters. If the portfolio-imbalance theory outlined above is correct, the banking system does periodically alternate between these two instruments as primary adjustment media, and it takes about five quarters for the system to go full cycle in this continuing process. Surely this is only one piece of evidence for that theory of the rate cycle. For the moment, it may be sufficient merely to note the existence of the cycle itself.

In summary, this section has attempted to analyze the nature of the relationships between the Federal funds rate and the Treasury bill rate. It has been shown that the two instruments are very close substitutes, so long as bank portfolios do not become too far out of line with the desired composition. When that happens, as can be expected in the normal course of responses to changes in monetary policy, the costs of portfolio imbalance will come into play so as to generate a cyclical movement in the difference between the two interest rates. This cycle will vary in amplitude as the strength and persistance of the policy actions vary; but it exhibits over the past decade a stable periodicity of about five calendar quarters.

---

1. $k = 2m/j = (2 \times 117)/3 = 78$ weeks.

Chapter Three. Trading Volume

Introduction

The price (interest rate) of Federal funds and the volume of transactions are determined simultaneously by the interaction of supply and demand in the market for borrowed reserves, as illustrated in the preceding
chapter. But the volume figure has a life of its own and is interesting
to the analyst for several reasons. First, policy decisions of different
types can cause an increase in the interest rate on Federal funds to be
accompanied either by an increase or a decrease in the volume of transactions. Second, the role of the volume figures has been misunderstood by
a number of writers on the subject, many of whom have denied the existence
of such a role. And third, there is a plurality of figures on trading volume which must be sifted before a meaningful data series can be found.

The market description of the previous chapter is recalled in Figure 7.
Point A (upper diagram) represents an initial equilibrium at which the
funds rate is equal to the discount rate. An increase in the latter would
cause the supply curve to shift to S_2, bringing a new equilibrium at point
B. Interest rates rise, but the reduced supplies at each rate cause volume to fall from Q_a to Q_b. On the other hand, an increase in credit demands or a decrease in reserve availability (tightening of open-market rather than discount policy) probably will cause rates to rise, but volume
could do anything. If the thrust of the tightening is felt at those banks
which are primarily buyers of funds, then the main effect may be an increase in demand for funds. Consider the movement from points B to C;
there is little or no effect on the rate, but there is a substantial increase in the volume of transactions. On the other hand, a tightening of
policy which is felt throughout the system will shift the supply schedule
to the left. In the extreme case in which there is no effect on the demand for funds, there would be a movement along the demand curve, as from
point D to E (lower diagram). Note that if the market started at point A,
that type of supply shift, involving constant discount policy, would have

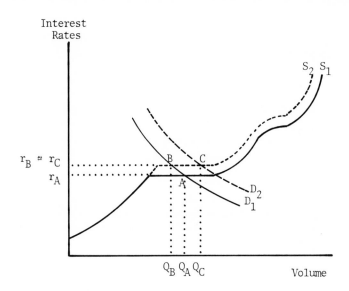

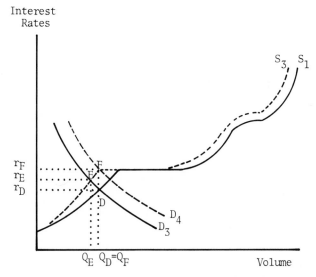

Figure 7. Volume Effects of Shifts
in the Supply and Demand Schedules

no effect on the equilibrium solution unless it were large enough to move
the market into the inelastic range of supply. A more likely effect of a
change in general policy would be a shift in both demand (D_3 to D_4) and
supply (S_1 to S_3). Depending on relative elasticities the volume figure
corresponding to point F could be equal to, below, or above the initial
equilibrium. Thus if some valid meaning can be attached to this volume
figure, it will be interesting to examine these elasticities more closely.

Some writers have denied any importance to volume. Typical of this
group is William R. Poole, who in a paper on stochastic reserve flows wrote
that "the volume of Federal funds trading appears to be a relatively useless piece of information."[1] Other writers such as George W. McKinney
have assigned almost mystical properties to the market. McKinney's book
on discount window administration argues that Federal funds

> borrowing brings about a more efficient utilization of the total
> volume of Federal Reserve credit outstanding, without changing the
> total of such credit outstanding. This increased efficiency permits
> the banking system to operate on a smaller reserve base and, inci-
> dentally, permits the Federal Reserve System to operate on a smal-
> ler portfolio of Governments.[2]

Similar statements, ignoring the effects of price changes and possibly
perverse reactions to policy changes, fill the literature. A thorough
critique of both lines of reasoning is given in Part Two of the present
study.[3]

Does Volume Make Any Real Difference?

The various relationships discussed in the preceding chapter provide
some clues as to how changes in the volume of trading should properly be
regarded. Three concepts come to mind. First, Federal funds are secondary reserves to the lenders. Second, these funds increase the available
reserves of borrowers. Third, if the combination of these two effects increases the ratio of active to idle reserve balances, the velocity of total
reserves will be increased. Each of these points will be considered in
turn.

---

1. "Commercial Bank Reserve Management in a Stochastic Model: Implications for Monetary Policy," Journal of Finance, XXIII (December, 1968),
776.

2. The Federal Reserve Discount Window: Administration in the Fifth
District (New Brunswick, New Jersey: Rutgers University Press, 1960), p.54.

3. See especially Chapter IV, pp. 79-99.

When a bank sells Federal funds, it is making a short-term loan which
it will then regard as a secondary reserve. If the loan were not made and
no other arrangements were made for disposing of the funds, the bank would
merely hold idle reserves earning no interest. The crucial point, of
course, is whether some other arrangements would or would not have been
made. Does the Federal funds market serve the lenders as a substitute for
idle funds or simply as a substitute for some other form of secondary reserves? If the latter, then we must go a step further. The choice becomes one of selling funds or perhaps buying a Treasury bill. The decision
is made to sell funds. Had the bill been bought, it probably would have
been acquired from a dealer in government securities; whether or not this
dealer were a member bank, it would have been paid with Federal funds
(i.e., immediate credit) in exchange for the bill.[1] This credit could be
viewed as releasing the dealer from the necessity of borrowing Federal
funds from a New York (or other) bank. If we designate this hypothetical
bank as Bank B and our original bill buyer as Bank A, the effects of these
transactions can be summarized through abstracted balance sheets. If Bank
A buys the Treasury bill from a dealer, the following changes will occur:[2]

Bank A		Dealer		Bank B	
Reserves -		Bills -		Reserves +	
Bills +		Federal		FF Sold -	
		Reserve			
		draft +			

On the other hand, the direct sale of Federal funds will bring these
changes:

Bank A		Bank B	
Reserves -		Reserves +	FF
FF Sold +			Purchased +

The effect on Bank A's balance sheet is altered little by the choice. But
the other bank is affected, having in the one case merely exchanged one
asset for another, while in the other case having increased its scale of

1. Member-bank dealers would receive payment in the form of a credit
to their deposit accounts at the Reserve Bank. Non-bank dealers would be
paid by negotiable Federal Reserve drafts. See Ira O. Scott, Government
Securities Market (New York: McGraw-Hill, 1965), pp. 101-102.

2. The following diagrams are standard condensed balance sheets,
with assets to the left of each divider and liability accounts to the
right. The notation FF refers to the volume of Federal funds transacted.

operation by the act of borrowing. For the banking system the supply of
reserves is unaltered under either alternative. Yet the scale of the system's operation is directly increased by the reserve transfer, although not
by the bill transfer. The reason for this paradox is clear. When a bank
buys a Treasury bill, it is completing nothing more than a transfer of
assets. But when it sells Federal funds, it is creating a loan liability
within the system. This is the essential difference between transferring
funds and creating funds.

In saying this, we do not get very far. Reserves are unchanged; deposits are unchanged; total loans to those outside the banking system are
unchanged. Only total assets and liabilities have increased, a fact which
is little more than a statistical anomaly as long as we are careful to keep
the point in mind in selecting an indicator for changes in bank credit.

Now let us change the assumptions of the example slightly. The crucial
characteristic of the first case was that all of the funds being pushed
around were in motion and working already. To alter the results some means
is needed for drawing idle funds into activity. That means may be found in
the interest rate. The argument implicit here is that the demand for or
the supply of money will, for at least some persons or firms, be interest-
elastic because of the changing opportunity costs of holding idle transactions balances. Keynes in the General Theory denied such an effect,[1]
but it is well established under modern analysis. As Ronald M. Teigen
summarized the point,

> Assuming that the transactions for which balances are held are spread
> out evenly over the period between income receipts so that the aver-
> age transactions balance which is held over the period is not trivi-
> ally small, it may be profitable to invest part of the inflow of in-
> come until it is needed for transacting, at which time the asset may
> be reconverted into cash. Whether or not such activity is profitable
> depends, of course, on the rate of interest available on liquid
> assets compared with the cost of buying and selling securities.[2]

1. John Maynard Keynes, The General Theory of Employment, Interest,
and Money (London: Harcourt, Brace & Co., 1936), p. 196.

2. "The Demand for and Supply of Money," Readings in Money, National
Income, and Stabilization Policy, Warren L. Smith and Ronald M. Teigen
(eds.), (Homewood, Ill.: Richard D. Irwin, 1965), p. 55. The argument itself was developed in William J. Baumol, "The Transactions Demand for Cash:
an Inventory-Theoretic Approach," Quarterly Journal of Economics, LXVI
(November, 1952), 545-556; and in James Tobin, "The Interest-Elasticity of
the Transactions Demand for Cash," Review of Economics and Statistics,
XXXVIII (August, 1956), 241-247.

Teigen goes on to cite several studies of this interest-elasticity, most
of which result in demand elasticities of from -0.6 to -0.9.[1] His own estimation finds a much smaller demand elasticity but a high supply elasticity.
As will be shown momentarily, either elasticity being very much different
from zero will imply that the banking system can change interest rates on
highly liquid assets and successfully attract idle balances.

Suppose that a corporation is holding idle cash balances. Unfortunately, it is highly unlikely that these balances will be in the form of currency; they instead will be demand deposits at a commercial bank. When
interest rates on Treasury bills rise, the corporation may be induced to
transfer part of its deposit into bills by purchasing securities from its
bank. The latter's required reserve--but not its reserve balance--de-
clines, and the bank becomes in the position of having excess reserves
which can be sold in the Federal funds market. The line of causation in
this example might work as follows. When credit demands rise at major
banks, those banks may increase their offering rates for Federal funds. As
other banks seek to acquire funds to sell at the higher rates, selling
pressure will develop in the bill market, driving interest rates up. Idle
funds outside the banking system are activated to take advantage of these
higher rates. Ultimately these funds pass through the Federal funds market. The effects on balance sheet accounts are shown below, where a 12%
reserve requirement is used for illustration.

Bank A	
Required Reserves -12	Demand Deposits -100
FF Sold +12	
Bills -100	

Bank B			Public	
Reserves +12	FF Purchased +12		Bills +100	
			Deposits -100	

The process does not stop here. Bank B has excess reserves which it
bought in order to make new loans. Under conditions of monetary stress,
conditions which led to the initial rate increase, nearly-maximum credit
expansion can be expected from the increase in excess reserves. That is,
the banking system will continue to make new loans as long as it has excess
reserves. When this process has been completed, the original 100 asset

---

1. Teigen, "The Demand for and Supply of Money," p. 52.

units which had been held in bills will have been converted into new loans, and total assets and liabilities will have been increased only by the amount of the transfer of Federal funds (12 units). The only difference between this case and the earlier example is that the banking system has in a roundabout way converted secondary reserves into business loans. Such roundaboutness was necessary because the Treasury bill was sold in such a way that the sale did not involve reserve funds; the seller had to reduce its holdings of secondary reserves, rather than being able to convert immediately to the desired assets.

One more example will complete the picture. The increase in interest rates may induce banks to give up part of their cushion of excess reserves by watching their reserve positions more closely and trimming the fat more frequently and more accurately. As described in Chapter I (pp. 15-18), there are costs involved in this operation; the rate increase makes it easier for banks to cover these costs. The transferral of these reserves from idle to active accounts has exactly the same effect on credit expansion as an actual increase in reserves. Those banks which are in a position to put funds to work gain reserves, and nothing is lost to the other banks. The latter have traded excess primary reserves for a secondary reserve asset. Total loans and deposits will rise by a multiple of the transferred sum until a new equilibrium is reached.

There are, then, three possible results from an increase in the volume of Federal funds transactions.

1. The increase may result from Federal funds becoming more attractive than alternative forms of short-term investment without any change in anyone's liquidity preference. The sum total of active balances is not affected by the transaction. The only change in the aggregate balance sheet of the banking system is that total assets and liabilities rise by the amount of the increase in funds volume. There is no expansion of deposits or loans.

Banking System	
FF Sold + 100	FF Purchased +100
Assets + 100	Liabilities +100

2. The increase may be effected through the operation of an interest-elastic demand for money: a rise in the interest rate on securities reduces the public's willingness to hold idle deposits. The holding of secondary reserve assets shifts from the banking system to the public, reduc-

ing the reserve balance required and permitting the banking system to convert its security holdings into active loans. There still is no multiple
credit expansion.

Banking System

FF Sold +100	FF Purchased +100	
Loans +833		
Bills -833		
Assets +100	Liabilities +100	

3. The increase may be effected through an interest-elastic supply of
money, as the banking system conserves its own cash resources in response
to the rate increase. Idle reserves are put to work, directly increasing
the ability of the system to support new loans on existing reserves. Deposits increase along with loans, and the scale of the system increases.

Banking System

FF Sold +100	FF Purchased +100	
Loans +833	Deposits +833	
Excess Reserves -100		
Required Reserves +100		
Assets +933	Liabilities +933	

If we seek to give a proper interpretation to changes in trading volume, it would be very nice to know which of these situations will dominate
actual circumstances. The findings of Ronald Teigen, referred to above,
provide some insight into this problem. Using quarterly data for 1946 IV
to 1959 IV, he finds that most of the interest-elasticity observed in the
stock of money comes from the supply rather than the demand side, the for-
mer elasticity being about 0.2 and the latter -0.05.[1] Both of these figures are low, however, and lend some credence to the view that changes in
volume are little more than distributional effects, as in the first case
above. A fuller study of these problems must await the second part of
this work.

Asset Transformation and the
Velocity of Reserves

Whenever the Federal funds market is successful in attracting idle
funds into active use, the effective reserve base of the system is increased.

---

1. *Ibid.*, p. 64.

Consequently the volume of loans and deposits sustainable by the same level of total reserves increases by a multiple of the volume of new funds. This process may be regarded as involving an increase in the velocity, rather than the volume, of reserves. Just as changes in the velocity of money are substitutable for changes in the available quantity of money to the consuming public, so these effects on reserve velocity are substitutable for changes in the quantity supplied.

Using the term "velocity" to describe the ratio between bank assets (or bank loans or deposits) and reserves may be a bit unsettling. Reserves do not move much at all; they mostly just sit in vaults and in ledgers at Reserve Banks. Unlike money, which passes from hand to hand in the process of virtually all economic transactions, reserves for the most part sit idle. Nonetheless, reserves are used as backing for multiple deposits. At any moment each dollar of reserves is pledged, as it were, to several dollars of deposits. If all the customers of a bank demanded to exchange their deposits for cash, the ratio of deposits to reserves would indeed indicate how fast these reserves would have to circulate in order to keep the bank in business. That is to say, reserves have a potential, though not an actual, velocity, and it is this potential figure in which we are interested. Never mind that in the case just cited the reserves would be unable to circulate above a unit velocity and the bank would be driven into bankruptcy by this sluggishness. The soundness of the fractional reserve system hopefully permits us to abstract from that unpleasant contingency.[1]

If the banking system never held excess reserves, the velocity of total reserves, respecting the total volume of deposits, would always be equal to the reciprocal of the average reserve requirements established by the Federal Reserve.[2] Velocity could be derived from the system's reserve identity as follows:

$$RES_R \equiv RRR_{CRC} \cdot DD_{CRC} + RRR_{RC} \cdot DD_{RC} + RRR_{CN} \cdot DD_{CN} + RRR_{TD} \cdot TD, \qquad (1)$$

---

1. The velocity concept is used here in preference to the reciprocal measure, "financial multipliers," in order to focus on the similarities with monetary velocity and to differentiate changes in velocity from changes in the levels supplied.

2. Here, as elsewhere, the existence of nonmember banks is ignored. The quantitative importance of this omission, especially with regard to the funds market, is surely negligible.

where RES_R = required reserves (= total reserves)
RRR = required reserve ratio
CRC = central reserve city banks
RC = reserve city banks
CN = country banks
DD = demand deposits
TD = time deposits.

Equation (1) reflects most of the different classifications traditionally used by the Federal Reserve in applying discriminatory reserve requirements against different classes of banks and deposits. Since 1966 several additional classifications have been made, but they may be ignored for the moment. The point here is to illustrate that the ratio of total deposits to total reserves is a complex function, even when excess reserves are excluded. The Federal Reserve could not peg velocity at any given level unless it were able to offset changes in the distribution of deposits by deftly-timed changes in requirements. Alternatively it could end the practice of applying discriminatory requirements, but so far it has chosen not to do so. Recognizing that "average reserve requirements" are a function both of Federal Reserve policy and of the distribution of deposits among banks and among classes of deposits within each bank, we can proceed to measure velocity.

$$RES_R = r \cdot D, \text{ or } V = \frac{1}{r} = \frac{D}{RES_R} , \tag{2}$$

where r = average reserve requirements,
D = total deposits,
V = deposit velocity of reserves,

and where we still assume away the existence of excess reserves. Dropping that assumption requires one minor modification:

$$V = \frac{D}{RES_T} = \frac{D}{RES_R + RES_E} = \frac{D}{rD + RES_E} , \tag{3}$$

dividing total reserves into required and excess components. Euqation (3) shows that velocity will be a function of average reserve requirements and the ratio of deposits to excess reserves. More simply, it would be expressed as a non-linear function of average requirements and the ratio of excess to total reserves. Maximum velocity would be reached only when there were no excess reserves and all deposits were concentrated where they would have minimum reserve requirements. In practice, velocity will fluctuate with changes in interest rates on Federal funds and Treasury bills

(influencing excess reserves) and on time deposits (influencing the distribution of deposits).[1]

In addition to deposit velocity, two related measures are of interest.
Asset velocity measures the ability of reserves to sustain total bank assets. But this measure is of no practical relevance, since total assets
can make capricious changes not related to credit expansion, such as the
Type One Federal funds transfer in the preceding section (p. 66). Loan
velocity, on the other hand, is of considerable interest. This figure may
be approximated if we assume that deposits on the liability side will
equal reserves plus loans plus investments on the asset side; this approxi-
mation abstracts from peculiarities arising from capital stock, borrowings,
bank premises, and the like that could be included easily but which would
only clutter the present exposition. Now let

L = total loans

S = security holdings (investments)

V_L = loan velocity of reserves

and V_S = securities velocity of reserves.

Then

$$V = \frac{D}{rD + RES_E} = \frac{L + S + RES_T}{rD + RES_E} = \frac{L + S}{rD + RES_E} + 1, \qquad (4)$$

so that V_L and V_S may be derived through definitions similar to those
yielding total velocity, or deposit velocity, V. Furthermore,

$$V = V_L + V_S + 1, \qquad (5)$$

the "1" on the end representing the "reserve velocity" of reserves. The
only reason that this terminology is of interest here is that any shift in
assets between loans and investments obviously increases the ability of the
reserve base to sustain loans.[2] As illustrated by the Type Two Federal

----

1. This velocity function is quite similar in concept to a relation developed by Teigen to explain the ratio of actual deposits to maximum deposits. The usual expression of the function in econometric studies either
states that free reserve levels are a function of short-term interest rates
or that some short-term rate is a function of bank reserve positions.
Teigen's exposition may be found in his "Demand and Supply Functions for
Money in the United States: Some Structural Estimates," Econometrica, XXXII
(October, 1964), 476-509; and, in somewhat revised form, in "An Aggregate
Quarterly Model of the U.S. Monetary Sector, 1953-1964," Targets and Indica-
tors of Monetary Policy, Karl Brunner (ed.), (San Francisco: Chandler, 1969).

2. The importance of this particular multiplier was suggested by Warren Smith in "On the Effectiveness of Monetary Policy." The point is fully
developed in Ronald A. Shearer, "The Expansion of Bank Credit: an Alternative Approach," Quarterly Journal of Economics, LXXVII (August, 1963),
485-502.

funds transfer, in which there was no change in deposits but only a shift
of secondary reserves into loans, this may usefully be described as an increase in the loan velocity of the reserve base.

Tying together some loose ends: three types of Federal funds transfers
have been described, differentiated by the means by which funds are at-
tracted into the market. The effects of each on the aggregate balance
sheet of the banking system have already been described. To that may now
be added their effects on reserve velocity, which is merely another way,
perhaps a little clearer, of describing the same result. The first type
of transfer causes asset velocity to rise, while deposit and loan velocit-
ies are unaffected. The second type brings an increase in loan and asset
velocity, although the deposit ratio is still constant. The third type,
the only one in which idle bank reserves are actually reduced, increases
all three types of velocity.

The Problem of Measurement

The volume of trading in this market is not easily measured. An unambiguous figure would require data on each single transaction, regardless
of the method of consummation, listing both buyer and seller. And even
then an arbitrary definition would have to be adopted to separate transactions made for purposes unrelated to the loan market.

Several different efforts have been made over the years to estimate
total volume. Bernice Turner's 1930 book on the funds market made no attempt to use actual figures. Two years later Benjamin H. Beckhart and
James G. Smith, in their book on the New York money market, presented the
following estimate:

> The volume of Federal funds handled in the money market in any
> one day ranges up to 250 millions of dollars, with 100 millions of
> dollars representing a normal day's trading. The volume handled nat-
> urally mounts on the settlement days, Tuesdays and Fridays, inasmuch
> as the greatest demand for Federal funds arises from banks desirous
> of adjusting their reserve balances. Some banks, however, adjust their
> position constantly, so that there is a continuous demand from this
> source.[1]

However, they cited no source for this information. It most likely was
derived from interviews with participating banks, as little information
was then available from published sources. Another possible reference

---

1. The New York Money Market: Sources and Movements of Funds (New
York: Columbia University Press, 1932), p. 42.

would have been the questionnaire sent by Congress in 1931 to each of the
Reserve Banks; part of that questionnaire dealt with the extent of trading
in Federal funds in the various districts, but it produced little more
than qualitative statements from most of the banks.[1]

The next time a volume figure appeared in print was in 1959, when the
Federal Reserve System published the results of its 1956 survey of large
bank participation. The state of the art at that time was summarized in
one brief table:[2]

period	average daily volume of transactions ($ millions)
1925 - 32	100 - 250
1950 - 53	350 - 450
1955 - 57	800 - 1100

Again, no explicit sources were given, although the first figure obviously
was taken from Beckhart and Smith. The survey itself revealed that in
November, 1956, the surveyed banks purchased an average of about $600 mil-
lion per day.

From that point on, the situation began to improve. The three-year
survey starting in September, 1959, produced some fairly detailed volume
figures for major banks. These figures have been continued to the present
and today are published in each Federal Reserve Bulletin. Weekly averages
of daily figures are presented. The data are for 46 major reserve city
banks and are further divided by banks in New York, Chicago, and elsewhere.
The banks were selected on the basis of the three-year survey, which revealed that most of the money flowing through the market found its way to
at least one of these 46 banks.

> One conclusion from the 3-year study was that while a substantial
> and fluctuating number of banks around the country may enter the Fed-
> eral funds market on the selling side on any particular day, the group
> of banks that accounts for most of the purchases is relatively stable
> and relatively small. Thus, for the purpose of the Federal funds ser-
> ies, it was possible to reduce the number of reporting banks to 46 and
> still maintain a series that is an adequate indicator of Federal funds
> activity for current national money market analysis. During the 3-
> year survey period, using the purchases of all reporting banks as a
> close approach to the total volume of all transactions in the Federal

---

1. U.S. Senate, Committee on Banking and Currency, "Federal Reserve
Questionnaires," Hearings Before a Subcommittee Pursuant to S. Res. 71,
Appendix to Part Six (71st Cong., 3d sess., 1931), pp. 725-727.

2. Board of Governors, The Federal Funds Market, p. 33.

funds market, the purchases of these 46 banks accounted for four-fifths
of the purchases and their sales were equal to three-fifths of total
purchases.[1]

While this series clearly is an adequate indicator for some purposes,
such as measuring cycles in activity, it might understate market growth
over any length of time, as the number of participants increases along
with their trading volume. It also raises serious problems of double
counting. To illustrate both of these problems, the data for Sixth District banks in 1966 may be used, since they include all transfers of funds
involving district banks, and not just a selected sample. This survey indicated that banks in the Atlanta District purchased an average of $167
million per day and sold $149 million.[2] Clearly, there was a net inflow
of funds to the district. But how much money actually changed hands?
What volume of reserves was activated? To take an extreme case, suppose
that all district participants except one entered the market only to sell
funds, and they always sold to that one exception. That bank, in turn,
always sold any funds it received to a major New York bank. Suppose further that both the New York bank and the big Atlanta bank were included in
the sample of 46 daily funds reporters. If the Atlanta bank took in and
sold $100 million per day, then gross purchases reported in the Bulletin
would be twice that sum, or $200 million. A survey such as the one made
in 1966 would show District purchases to be $100 million and sales to be
$200 million. Every time the money turns over, it gets counted in the
figures again.

The problem is to select a sample which maintains over time a stable
portion of total volume, and then in some way to eliminate the double
counting of transfers going through one bank in the sample on its way to
another. If this can be done, then changes in the resulting measure will
reflect changes in the volume of funds moving through the market.

With regard to the first problem, the Atlanta data provide some support
for the validity of the 46-bank sample. Between 80% and 85% of both the
sales and the purchases of funds made by banks in the district appear to
have been made with banks included in the national sample. That figure
coincides well with the proportions cited above relating to the 1959-1962

---

1. Board of Governors, "New Series on Federal Funds," Federal Reserve
Bulletin, L (August, 1964); 946.

2. Brandt and Crowe, "The Federal Funds Market in the Southeast,"
p. 11.

period; the 46 banks are, if the Atlanta data are indicative of conditions throughout the country, maintaining their share of the action.

The remaining problem is to get rid of any double counting. This is done in the published series by netting out the transactions made by each individual bank over each reserve computation period. If a given bank both buys and sells the same amount of funds during the period, there will be no effect on its average reserve balance; so neither transfer should be counted in a measure of "activated balances." Such activity, which may reach considerable volumes at times, is really just noise in the series. It is listed in the Bulletin as "2-way transactions,"[1] and it includes not only the movement of funds through intermediaries but also the correction of mistakes resulting from uncertain reserve flows and the use of the market for speculative purposes in anticipation of rate changes during the period.

The appropriate figure to use for a data series is published as the net purchases of the net buying banks included in the sample. Some banks in the sample are net sellers at least part of the time, but it cannot be determined from available data whether their sales are made primarily to banks within or without the sample group. But the point is important. One cannot use the net purchases of the 46 banks as a group, because that figure nets out not only all net sales made to banks outside the sample (a figure which we would like to keep) but also all sales within the group; if reserves are "activated" within the sample group, this net purchases figure would fail to register the event. Taking instead the net purchases of those banks which were net purchasers is a far superior measure. It eliminates all double counting, and its only failing is that it omits the net purchases of all banks which are net purchasers but are not included in the sample. And it already has been shown that that sum seems to be a fairly stable portion of total activity in the market. This measure of volume will understate total volume by about 20%, but it should register both cyclical and secular movements in market activity. Movement in the series over the past decade is shown in Figure 8.

---

1. For an exposition of this series, see Board of Governors, "New Series on Federal Funds," pp. 951-952.

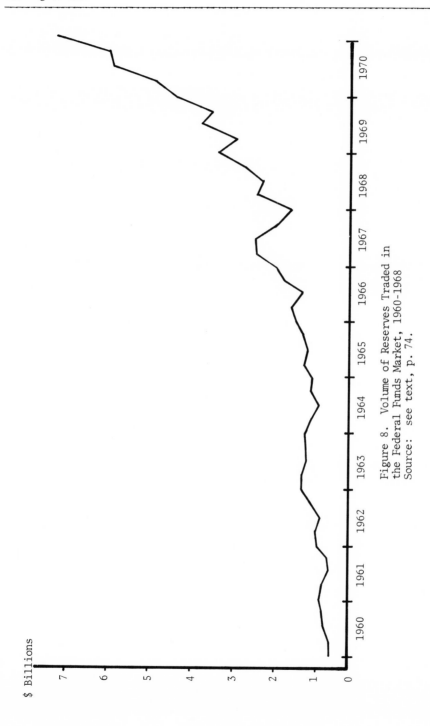

Figure 8. Volume of Reserves Traded in
the Federal Funds Market, 1960-1968
Source: see text, p. 74.

PART TWO. THE TRANSMISSION OF MONETARY POLICY

Chapter Four. A Catalogue of Hypotheses

The description just given of the Federal funds market has left open the question of the relationship that activity in the market might have to the transmission of monetary policy. The issue arose at several points. Chapter I concluded with the observation that the geographic flow of funds seems to spread policy actions throughout the country, taking pressure off the central money market where the initial impact of policy decisions usually is felt. On the other hand, this "spreading" action might diminish the total impact of any policy change. Chapter II detailed the possible effects that different types of policy decisions could have on both the volume of trading and the prevailing interest rate in the market but left open the question of which effects could be expected to dominate actual circumstances. Then Chapter III took up the issue of the effects that changes in trading activity could have on the extension of bank credit; again, the resolution of conflicting possibilities had to be left open. The purpose of Part Two of this work is to provide some more definitive answers to these questions. The present chapter surveys the various theories which have attempted formally to link the funds market to the policy transmission process. Then Chapter V presents a theoretical model of the policy process in order to provide a framework for testing hypotheses; the number of possible relationships is too great to be analyzed without recourse to a complete model which shows both the effects of monetary policy on the funds market and the effects of the market on general credit conditions. Finally, in Chapter VI, empirical tests are devised, using post-Accord data and an econometric model designed expressly for this purpose.

Formal models relating the Federal funds market to other monetary phenomena do not abound in the professional literature. There are, however, a number of fragmentary accounts of the various possible relationships. Most of these accounts fall into one of two schools of thought,

between which there has been almost no dialogue. The first school maintains that the funds market serves as an aid or a lubricant to the transmission of policy; the second, that it acts instead as an offset to policy
actions. In addition there are a few writers who have treated the market
as being related to policy transmission but who have not commented specifically on its net impact. Before a synthesis of these diverse hypotheses
can be developed, the original authors must be afforded the space to present their own views.

Development of the Concept of the Funds Market as an Aid to Policy

> The Federal Fund Market is an aid in carrying out the policies of
> the Federal reserve banks. When Funds are put into the Market, they
> might remain with an institution that had no particular use for them,
> were it not for the fact that there is a highly developed market in
> which they find their way to the centers where they are most needed
> for the day. Likewise, when the Federal reserve banks decide to
> tighten money through their open market operations, they can do so
> knowing that the Federal Funds so constantly in demand will be pur-
> chased from sources where they are least needed.[1]

So wrote Bernice C. Turner in 1930. The argument, as presented, is
rather sensible. Open market operations are conducted in the money market
centers, primarily in New York City. There the initial impact of any policy action is felt. Surely the funds market will help shift this impact to
banks around the country. When reserves are supplied to New York banks,
those funds can be sold to a San Francisco bank if the distribution of
credit demands warrants such a shift. Without the funds market, redistribution would take place through the natural spreading of deposits, as monetary transactions of all sorts occur in the course of the nation's work.[2]
Presumably this process is slower and less efficient than the action of
the funds market. Similarly, a tightening of policy in the money market
centers will bring a tightening throughout the country as the New York
banks seek to attract funds from other banks, reducing the abilities of
the latter to expand credit to their own customers.

A more cautious statement of this view came two years later from
Beckhart and Smith.

---

1. Turner, p. 96.

2. The regional lags in the effects of monetary policy are discussed
in Ira O. Scott, "The Regional Impact of Monetary Policy," Quarterly Journal of Economics, LXIX (May, 1955), 269-284.

Trading in Federal funds has permitted banks to figure more closely on their reserves and doubtless has been a factor in the paring of these down to a minimum. Inasmuch as the amount of excess reserves maintained is negligible, the purchase and sale of Federal funds does not relieve the banking system, however much it may relieve the individual bank, of the necessity of reliance on or borrowing from the Federal Reserve banks. Excess reserves of the banking system are so small that gold exports, increases in the amount of money in circulation, decreases in treasury currency, and appropriate changes in various items on the Federal Reserve statement of condition, will force increases in member bank borrowings. The purchase and sale of Federal funds, therefore, may simply be looked upon as a further refinement in the clearance mechanism, without having any more than a temporary effect on member bank borrowings.[1]

No evidence is offered in support of these contentions, but the argument itself is reasonable. If the excess reserves of the system are so small that increases in Federal funds volume will be unable to exert much leverage against the multiplier process wielded by the Federal Reserve, then the funds market will, as the authors imply, simply lubricate the "clearance mechanism," enabling policy actions to operate more fluidly. Beckhart and Smith viewed the policy mechanism as working through increases or decreases in the reliance of the system on borrowed reserves, a process to which the Federal Reserve itself seems to adhere at least part of the time. However, that concept is not at all central to the point made concerning the funds market, that free reserves cannot be much altered by market activity.

That argument has not lost sway in more recent years. George McKinney's 1960 book on the discount window contains this account of the role of the market:

Member bank borrowing from sources other than the Federal Reserve banks raises an interesting question as to how such borrowing influences the effectiveness of Federal Reserve credit policy. Interbank loans, regardless of form, generally involve a transfer of existing reserves from the lending bank to the borrowing bank, and do not (directly) affect either the total volume of bank reserves or the level of required reserves. Actually, the development of the Federal funds market and other non-Federal Reserve sources of member bank borrowing increases the effectiveness of credit policy actions. Such borrowing brings about a more efficient utilization of the total volume of Federal Reserve credit outstanding, without changing the total of such credit outstanding. This increased efficiency permits the banking system to operate on a smaller reserve base and, incidentally, permits the Federal Reserve System to operate with a smaller portfolio of governments. With the banking system generally operating more efficiently--that is with a smaller volume of excess reserves--any change

---

1. Beckhart and Smith, pp. 47-48. By "increases in the amount of money in circulation," they evidently intended "currency," not "money."

in open market policy will of necessity take hold that much sooner, for it will not be cushioned by a large volume of free reserves. Because the development of alternative sources of funds increases the over-all efficiency with which the banking system functions, it should be welcomed for that, if for no other, reason.[1]

Now this is an interesting argument. McKinney has gone beyond Beckhart and Smith's statement, for he has accepted the diminishing of the excess reserve cushion as a significant fact. But he ignores the process of the diminishment and argues that once the cushion has been reduced monetary policy should be able to work with less slippage. As long as activity in the funds market takes place at some constant rate, McKinney's argument holds. Thus there are two possibilities for the funds market to help policy-makers: if the effects of the market on excess reserves have no effect on the money multiplier (Beckhart and Smith) or if this effect occurs only in a gradual and predictable way so as not to offset the policy action when it is made (McKinney). McKinney, however, hedges somewhat with that parenthetic "directly" in the middle of his exposition. He seems to realize that there might occur an indirect expansion of bank deposits, raising the level of required reserves. The point is not pursued.

A similar argument is made by Dorothy Nichols, in her 1966 Technical Paper for the Board of Governors.

> The Federal funds market, by enabling an increasing number of banks to keep their funds fully invested, has helped to reduce short-run fluctuations in excess reserves as well as their average levels. It has also contributed to the development of a nationwide money market. Through this market the initial effects of Federal Reserve operations are more rapidly transmitted from the central money market to banks throughout the country and, through their impact on credit or money, or both, influence expenditures by the nonbank public.[2]

The only new dimension added here is the possibility of a reduction of short-run fluctuations in excess reserves. No figures are presented; if the statement is valid, however, then the case for the "lubrication" school has been strengthened. If policy changes are accompanied by changes in excess reserve levels that are either too large or too random to be offset by open-market operations, the efficacy of the policy action must be reduced.

On the other hand, it is a little difficult to visualize the response pattern implicit in Mrs. Nichols' argument. Because the funds market

---

1. McKinney, pp. 53-54. Quoted by permission of the publisher.

2. Nichols, Trading in Federal Funds, p. 8.

exists, banks hold smaller quantities of excess reserves and correspondingly greater quantities of highly-liquid secondary reserves in the form of Federal funds loans. Formerly, a tightening of monetary policy would result initially in a reduction of excess reserves rather than in the reduction in credit extension desired by policy officials. Mrs. Nichols' argument implies that because of the funds market banks no longer have this flexibility; they have already used up their degrees of freedom by eliminating the free reserve cushion. To the extent that the funds market provides an alternative cushion, i.e., the ability to convert secondary reserves and remaining excess primary reserves into earning assets more readily than would otherwise be possible, the argument loses its force.

It is apparent that Federal Reserve officials accept the view that the funds market acts as an aid to their work. In the first place, no effort has ever been made to hinder the operation of the market. Furthermore, the few public comments made on the subject by insiders have been consistent in support of that view: in addition to the arguments of Dorothy Nichols, several statements on this subject have been made by Parker Willis in his various writings on the funds market as an officer at the Federal Reserve Bank of Boston and as the chronicler of the market for the Board of Governors. He recently wrote that "the Federal funds market...has helped to distribute reserves supplied by the Federal Reserve."[1] And again, "Although transactions in Federal funds relieve the individual bank from use of the discount window, they do not relieve the banking system as a whole from reliance on the Federal Reserve."[2]

This school of thought, then, appears to be well established. We have seen that several prominent writers, both inside and outside official circles, have expressed various rationales for the existence of a positive relationship between policy actions and the Federal funds market. The crux of their argument is that short-run changes in trading activity will not be so large as to constitute an offset to the policy action, while long-run changes have been great enough to reduce the slippage that once resulted from variation in free reserve levels. Unfortunately, none of the writers in this school has tested for the possibility of sizable short-term perversity in trading volume. Not one seems to have considered the possibility

---

1. Parker B. Willis, A Study of the Market for Federal Funds (Washington: Board of Governors, 1967), p. 38.
2. Ibid., p. 32.

that banks might react to a tightening of policy by increasing their lendable funds through increased funds purchases. But lest these writers be
faulted too quickly for the omission, one must consider that their own
position has received the same lack of attention from the other side.

Development of the Counter-Argument:
the Funds Market as a Velocity-
Increasing Offset

One of the first authors to recognize the problems which might be
created by the trading of Federal funds was John Maynard Keynes.

> This gadget [non-price rationing of discount-window credit] has
> been rendered less effective of late (1929) by the growth of a prac-
> tice by which a member bank, which has not borrowed as much as it
> is entitled to, increases its discounts for the sole purpose of
> lending the reserve-resources thus obtained to other member banks,
> which have already borrowed from the Reserve Banks as much as they
> dare, at a rate which yields it a good profit over the Federal
> Reserve rate which it has paid. Resources transferred in this way
> from one member bank to another are called "Federal funds."[1]

It would be nice to know where Keynes got the idea that this practice was
widespread enough to render discount administration "less effective."
Beckhart and Smith have reported that the funds rate did indeed rise above
the discount rate during 1928 and 1929, sometimes by as much as a full percentage point,[2] so it could reasonably be surmised that a great deal of
reselling of funds might have occurred. This would imply that the Federal
Reserve banks had chosen to ration the credit extended to some individual
banks but not to attempt to prevent the emergence of a secondary market in
the funds lent by the discount department to other banks. Certainly they
could easily have prevented such a market from becoming widespread if they
had wanted, since most transactions then, as now, were transferred via the
Federal Reserve wire and thus were subject to scrutiny by discount officials. Today there is no doubt among bankers that borrowing from the Federal Reserve in order to make loans at a profit in the funds market will
result in a reprimand from the Reserve bank. Judging from Keynes' remark,
this was not true in the late Twenties.

---

1. John Maynard Keynes, A Treatise on Money (2 vols.; London: Mac-
Millan and Company, 1930), II, 242n.

2. Beckhart and Smith, pp. 46-47.

A more important point was raised some twenty-five years later, when
the post-war and post-Accord financial environment was beginning to assume
a recognizable form. This point was that monetary policy which attempted
to operate through control of the availability of credit or through the
supply of money might meet with one or several offsets in the form of velocity increases. Perhaps the best early treatment of this problem (dealing
not with the Federal funds market but with other types of secondary reserves) was presented by Warren L. Smith:

> The basic function of financial institutions is the mobilization of
> the financial resources of the economy in support of economic ac-
> tivity, and I suggest that when credit conditions are tightened and
> the creation of new money through the banking system is restricted,
> the financial machinery of the country automatically begins to work
> in such a way as to mobilize the existing supply of money more
> effectively, thus permitting it to do most of the work that would
> have been done by newly created money had credit conditions been
> easier.[1]

The specific problem with which Professor Smith was dealing was the
selling of Treasury bills by banks which had been holding them as secondary
reserves, to nonbank investors which had been holding idle balances with a
large interest elasticity. By increasing the ratio of active to idle deposits, the ability of a given reserve base to support business or other
loans would be increased. The presence of a large interest elasticity in
the liquidity preference schedules of the nonbank investors would be
essential to enable a small increase in bill rates to bring about a sizable
shift in security holdings. As evidence for this velocity reaction, Professor Smith considered the period of January through September of 1955.
Unborrowed reserves fell by $1.15 billion, reflecting a tightening of
monetary policy through open-market sales of government securities. This
decline was partially offset by increases in borrowing from the discount
window, and total reserves fell only by $550 million. The money supply was
reduced by $2.3 billion. During the same time period, however, commercial
and savings banks reduced their holdings of government securities by some
$7 billion, with the result that loans actually increased by about $8.9
billion. This was the largest percentage increase in bank loans for any
three-quarter period up to that time; the contractionary monetary policy

---

1. Smith, "On the Effectiveness of Monetary Policy," p. 601.

obviously had little effect on private credit expansion.[1]

In order to get rid of several billion dollars worth of government securities, the banking system had to cut prices and take a loss. During the nine month period, bill rates rose from 1.08% to 2.11%. Presumably this near-doubling of interest rates would sooner or later have slowed or halted the economic expansion, although, as Professor Smith observed, rates on loans rose only slightly and after a lag.[2] At any rate, the statistics of the period are powerful enough to warrant a close look at the possibility of a similar effect operating through the Federal funds market.

The first such look was taken by Professor Hyman Minsky in 1957. He began by taking exception to Smith's allegation that velocity-increasing offsets would occur "automatically" and "within an unchanging institutional framework."[3] He then argued that policy operations may induce "institutional evolution," shifting the relationships between instrument and target and producing effects "quite different from those desired."[4] He singled out two such changes for further study, one of which was the Federal funds market. Without providing any evidence of the importance of his argument, Minsky declared that "the federal funds market makes a given volume of reserves more efficient in supporting deposits." The point had, of course, been observed by others who with the same disdain for empiricism had assumed that the effect could not possibly be great enough or immediate enough to cause any problem for the operation of monetary policy and that, once the market had come of age, this increased efficiency would permit the policy mechanism to function more smoothly. But to Minsky it constituted a "basic change" in the system, a significant innovational response to monetary policy.

The more substantive part of Minsky's paper presents a formal rationale for the importance of institutional change in a financial model. He concedes that in a "stable institutional framework" increases in the

---

1. The statistics cited here are from the Federal Reserve Bulletin and are not exactly commensurate with those given by Smith. It must be kept in mind that the magnitudes are somewhat biased by the use of data for "all commercial and savings banks," unless one is willing to accept a broadened view of bank credit.

2. Smith, "On the Effectiveness of Monetary Policy," pp. 597-598.

3. Hyman P. Minsky, "Central Banking and Money Market Change," Quarterly Journal of Economics, LXXI (May, 1957), 172n.

4. Ibid., p. 172.

velocity of the money stock will be positively correlated with interest rates, so that any velocity-increasing activity will necessarily be incomplete; "tight money policy will be effective and the interest rate will rise to whatever extent is necessary in order to restrict the demand for financing to the essentially inelastic supply."[1] Then comes the heart of Minsky's analysis. When interest rates rise, the institutions have an increased incentive to conserve on their resources. If they can innovate so as to increase velocity without further increasing interest rates, the relationship between the two will shift. In fact, while the innovation is taking place, the relationship will become completely inelastic.

This whole argument, then, would seem to rest on the ability of the banking system to innovate whenever monetary policy tightens. It would be of no interest to the Federal Reserve in 1970 to be told that, when the national funds market evolved in the Fifties, the effectiveness of its policy decisions was temporarily reduced. But Minsky is not through yet. His next point is that shifts in the velocity-interest rate function reduce the liquidity of the system. Cash balances have been reduced, and the ability of the system to withstand shocks has been reduced. Minsky concludes that the central bank will be less able to prevent financial crises, so that the effectiveness of monetary policy has been severely weakened by the growth of the funds market.[2]

There really is no argument between Minsky and the adherents of the lubrication school on the way the funds market operates. Neither is concerned with the possibility of short-run changes in volume being used to affect velocity and therefore to offset policy actions, in the manner described by Warren Smith with respect to security holdings. The lubricationists believe that such activity would be limited by the narrow scope provided by free reserve levels in the banking system. Minsky, on the other hand, drew his conclusions on the belief that whatever the size of the volume offset, it probably would be accompanied by a sufficiently large increase in interest rates.

The quarrel between the two, if there is one, is over the significance of the increased efficiency of the reserve base brought about by the long-run growth of the funds market. The efficacy of monetary policy will be

---

1.   Ibid., p. 182.
2.   Ibid., p. 184.

increased if the banks are less able to react to policy changes by reducing
cash holdings. It will be hampered if this new inflexibility makes the
system so subject to crises that the central bank becomes unable or unwilling to undertake effective anti-inflationary actions. In the absence of
any supporting evidence, the Minsky thesis seems to be the work of a doomsday prophet.

The same thesis was updated and expanded in 1967 by one of Professor
Minsky's graduate students in a doctoral dissertation entitled "Causes and
Effects of Commercial Bank Innovation." The significance of that treatise
is that the author, Arnold Dill, separates the effects of the funds market
into "secular" and "cyclical" components. The secular effect is the innovational effect cited by Minsky; Dill describes it in much the same way
as his mentor, recognizing that the free reserve cushion is reduced and
claiming that the sensitivity of the system to crises is thereby increased.[1]
But he goes on to discuss the cyclical variation in market activity, showing that the size of the market is likely to move contracyclically to
policy changes. The evidence used by Dill is rather spotty. He considers
four post-Accord periods of monetary restraint and shows how the banking
system was able to reduce holdings of excess and secondary reserves as a
policy offset. A few figures on gross purchases of Federal funds are
cited in order to demonstrate that in the 1955 and 1966 contractions
growth in funds trading accompanied the decreases in reserve cushions.[2]
The implication is made that some sort of causal relation could be pre-
sumed to exist between the two series. Unfortunately, Dill does not present a clear statement of the way the funds market affects either desired
free reserve levels or loan expansion.

Still another view of the relationship between the market and policy
transmission is provided by Professors Karl Brunner and Allan Meltzer in a
1964 staff study prepared for the House Banking and Currency Committee. In
the course of a discussion of the role of free reserves in the policy process, Brunner and Meltzer distinguish between policy changes which bankers
view as temporary and those which they view as permanent. When free reserve levels change, bankers, it is argued, will at first think that the
change is only temporary, being due to some non-policy change in the

1. Arnold A. Dill, "Causes and Effects of Commercial Bank Innovation,"
Ph.D. dissertation, Washington University, 1967, pp. 69-70.

2. Ibid., pp. 74-79.

central bank's asset position. The newly-created excess reserves either
will be held as idle balances for a few days or will be lent in the Federal funds market. After a period of about three weeks the bankers will
realize that the increase is permanent, and they will increase loan volume.
"Modifications of reserve positions interpreted as only transitory will
not induce the portfolio adjustments typically associated with changes in
reserve positions deemed to be persistent and systematic."[1]

This argument is stated by Brunner and Meltzer in terms of easing of
policy; it is not at all clear that the response would be symmetric if
policy were tightened. But a more substantive problem is in the authors'
conception of the role of the funds market. They obviously believe that
selling excess reserves in the funds market has substantially the same
effect as holding the funds idle. "Banks receiving increased reserves may
hold them for a day or more, or lend them in the Federal funds market
rather than purchase securities or reduce loan rates to stimulate borrowing."[2] If the funds are held idle, the Brunner-Meltzer conception holds
without question. If the funds are sold in the open market, however, they
will be purchased by some bank which presumably will use them to finance
loan expansion at least indirectly. To the extent that the existence of
the funds market reduces the desire of the banks to hold idle balances
when they think the change in reserves is temporary, the market should act
as an aid to the Federal Reserve in easing policy, rather than as a deter-
rent as implied by Brunner and Meltzer.

The theses presented by Minsky, Dill, and Brunner and Meltzer to the
effect that the Federal funds market serves primarily as an offset to monetary policy fall short of the possibilities suggested by Warren Smith in
1956. If the funds market is to offset restrictive policy actions in any
regular way, then banks must be able to increase the velocity of the reserve base in one or more of the ways described above in Chapter III without inducing a large increase in interest rates. That is, banks must be
able through a small change in interest rates to induce a large change in
the quantity of funds being offered. Professor Smith's remarks were

---

1. Karl Brunner and Allan H. Meltzer, The Federal Reserve's Attach-
ment to the Free Reserve Concept: A Staff Analysis, Subcommittee on
Domestic Finance of the House Committee on Banking and Currency (88th
Cong., 2d sess., 1964), p. 15.

2. Ibid.

directed to another problem, that of reduction of secondary reserve levels
through sales of Treasury bills. But the argument would seem to be directly applicable to the funds market, as long as the existing levels of free
reserves are not so small that they cannot be still further reduced. Even
in that case it might still be feasible for the funds market to be used to
increase velocity; banks in relatively static areas could be induced
through interest rate changes to convert their secondary reserve portfolios
out of, say, Treasury bills and into Federal funds with the effect of the
system's aggregate portfolio being shifted out of government securities
into business loans. That, of course, would be the same effect postulated
by Warren Smith.

In order for the velocity-increasing offset thesis to be tested adequately, it must be shown not only that the volume of trading moves contracyclically but also that this movement has a stimulating effect on credit
expansion, which in turn requires either that the growth can be generated
through a small increase in interest rates or that credit demands will be
relatively inelastic to changes in interest rates. Warren Smith's exposition was built on the premise that even if money market rates rose sharply
(recalling that bill rates doubled in nine months in his case history),
lending rates would be much stickier because of the prevalence of non-
price credit rationing by the banking system. During the 1955 contraction,
rates charged for business loans were virtually constant. None of the
writers describing the Federal funds market as a policy offset have considered the significance of this effect.

Other Views on the Role of the Market

In addition to those who have explicitly treated the question of
whether the funds market helps or hinders the conduct of monetary policy,
there are two major papers which deal with the relationship of the market
to policy in different contexts. The first is A. James Meigs' book on
free reserves, in which a model of bank behavior is presented. The second
is a paper by William R. Poole on stochastic reserve flows.

The Meigs model starts with a definition of free reserves for an individual bank:[1]

---

1. Meigs, p. 43. The notation has been changed to conform with the
models developed below.

$$RES_F^i = RES_E^i + (D_{DF}^i - D_{DT}^i) + (FF_S^i - FF_P^i) - RES_B^i. \qquad (6)$$

Free reserves (RES_F) at the $\underline{i}$th bank are equal to the bank's excess reserves (RES_E) less its borrowings from the Federal Reserve (RES_B); plus the excess of its deposits placed at ("due from") other member banks (D_{DF}) over the deposits placed with it by ("due to") member banks (D_{DT}); plus the excess of its Federal funds sold (FF_S) over its Federal funds purchased (FF_P). The equation is a little strange. Ignoring the interbank deposit terms for the moment, the equation defines not the free reserve position but what the Federal Reserve calls the "basic" reserve position of the bank, the position that the bank would have had had it not borrowed either from the discount window or from member banks and had it not lent any funds to other banks. It is questionable whether funds acquired through the funds market should be classified as non-free to the individual bank, along with funds acquired from the central bank. The latter are obtained with the understanding that they are not to be used for credit expansion, but only to cover temporary deficits. They are to be repaid quickly. No such restrictions apply to Federal funds. Furthermore, funds sold in the market should no longer be regarded as free reserves. They are properly to be considered as secondary reserves until maturity.

Meigs' rationale for including both the Federal funds terms and the interbank deposits is that changes in either account provide immediate credit to the bank in the event of adverse clearings;[1] true enough, but so do changes in holdings of government securities, transactions in which are settled typically by Federal Reserve draft.[2] In fact, a much stronger case could be made for including Treasury bills in the equation; interbank deposits are held primarily as payment for correspondent services rendered, the amount being determined by mutual agreement between the two banks, and not, for the most part, by immediate considerations on the reserve position.[3] Faced with a reserve deficit, it would seem likely that the Federal

---

1. Ibid.

2. "Payments for trades in securities maturing in more than one year are generally made by bank check in clearing house funds, while trades in shorter term issues are generally made with Federal funds.... Approximately 80 per cent of all government security transactions are paid for in Federal funds." Gidge, pp. 44-45.

3. These relationships are discussed in Katherine Finney, Interbank Deposits: The Purpose and Effects of Domestic Balances, 1934-54 (New York: Columbia University Press, 1958), pp. 1-20.

funds market and the bill portfolio would be examined first. If the bank
maintained its correspondent balances at the agreed levels, these balances
would not be a ready source of reserve funds.[1] And in any case, no meaning whatever can be attached to the net position in interbank deposits,
which is the figure used by Meigs.

Using this contrived definition of free reserves, Meigs next postulates
a desired free reserve position for each bank,

$$RES_F^{*i} = f(DD^i, TD^i, RM_m, RM_{FRB}),$$ (7)

where RM_m = some market-determined interest rate. Desired free reserves
are a function of the level of demand (DD) and time (TD) deposits at the
individual bank and of market interest rates and the discount rate (RM_{FRB}).
Meigs further assumes that this function will be linearly homogeneous with
respect to demand plus time deposits, so that

$$\left(\frac{RES_F^i}{DD^i + TD^i}\right)^* = g(RM_m, RM_{FRB}).$$ (8)

This formulation implies first of all that the desired liquidity function
of the bank will be independent of the distribution of its deposits between
demand and time accounts, and second that it will be independent of the
level of reserve requirements. A shift out of demand and into time deposits not only should reduce the demand for liquidity because of the
greater stability of time deposits, it also would reduce the average reserve requirement faced by the bank, so that a given level of free reserves would represent a greater "cushion" against the bank's expected
variance in its reserve account. Similar reasoning would apply for changes
in the Federal Reserve's required reserve ratios. These considerations
suggest that the desired free reserve functions would be homogeneous not in
deposit levels but in the level of required reserves (RES_R). That is,

$$\left(\frac{RES_F^i}{RES_R^i}\right)^* = g'(RM_m, RM_{FRB}).$$ (9)

To return to Meigs' outline, the next step is to aggregate the function
over the banking system. Fortunately his troublesome entries in the individual bank free reserve definition cancel out in aggregation, leaving

---

1. Recalling the case study of Chapter I (pp. 15-18), the bank's
reserve position for the day was increased by $300,000 when that amount
was transferred from a correspondent balance to bring the latter in line
with the agreed balance. The reserve account then was adjusted by a sale
of Federal funds.

the standard definition of the term, $RES_F = RES_E - RES_B$. Then the function g is aggregated by summing the individual desired levels. The only new wrinkle is that a portmanteau variable is added, to allow for the influence of all factors other than interest rates:

$$\left(\frac{RES_F}{DD+TD}\right)^* = f(RM_m, RM_{FRB}, u). \tag{10}$$

For purposes of empirical estimation, Meigs assumes that the contents of u will be fairly constant over time, so that the equation can be estimated using only the interest rates. Having done so, he observes that some shifting of the function did occur during the estimation period, the shift having both cyclical and secular components. Meigs cites a number of possible causes of this pattern, among them the Federal funds market. "Development of the Federal funds market over the period [1954-1958] may have reduced the volume of excess reserves the banks want to hold at any given interest rate."[1]

To date the Meigs model is one of the most explicit statements of the role of free reserves in the monetary framework. It poses rather than answers some interesting questions about the role of the funds market. These are the same questions around which the other writers on the subject have been groping. If the market has caused a shift in the free reserve function, what implications does this have for policy transmission? Is the funds market related to the cyclical pattern found in the function? Meigs himself concludes that the cycle in free reserve demand is mostly seasonal (or monthly) in nature,[2] but he leaves open the question of what sort of process is generating the seasonal variation.

A completely different approach is taken by William R. Poole. His paper is designed to explain among other things "the significance of...the Federal funds market,"[3] in the context of a "stochastic inventory model" of bank reserve management. Poole fails to recognize the reserve-conserving possibilities of the market, a failure which leads him into a false conception of the role of trading volume. He argues that it is impossible for the banking system to make reserve adjustments through the market, "since the sum of all demands for Federal funds must be zero."[4] This

---

1. Meigs, p. 82.
2. Ibid., p. 78.
3. Poole, p. 770.
4. Ibid, p. 771.

curious statement is a consequence of treating the supply schedule for Federal funds as a "negative demand," and it leads to the conclusion that "the volume of Federal funds trading appears to be a relatively useless piece of information."[1] This decision permits Poole to concentrate his analysis on the interest rate pattern and to ignore volume changes. Fortunately it does not greatly bias his results.

A model is formulated in which it is assumed that each bank, in attempting to meet its reserve requirement, faces the following problem. It is the last day of the reserve period. During the day, stochastic changes are occurring in the reserve account. The bank must react so as to meet the requirement, and it has two choices in this model. At noon, it can go into the money market (represented by the funds market) and either borrow or lend funds as needed. Then the market closes. If, after that time, the reserve balance changes so as to create a deficit, the bank must go to the Federal Reserve and borrow at the discount rate. It is assumed that the funds rate will be below the discount rate and that the latter will represent the true cost of borrowing from the discount window. This last assumption may be dropped without much difficulty. Note that the possibility of a reserve flow occurring after the discount window closes is not considered. That makes it impossible for the bank to end up with a reserve deficit for the period and be subject to the more severe cost of being fined by the Federal Reserve.

The assumption that the bank chooses between going to the funds market and going to the discount window leads to a cost function associated with the bank's expected reserve flows. This total cost is equal to the expected reserve excess times the opportunity cost of holding excess balances (the Federal funds rate), plus the expected deficiency times the cost of waiting to borrow until after the funds market closes (the discount rate less the funds rate). By varying the volume of net purchases of Federal funds, the bank can minimize this sum. The result of this minimization is that the bank should act so as to set the probability of having a reserve deficit equal to the ratio of the Federal funds rate to the unit cost of

---

1. Ibid., p. 776. Analytically, Poole has confused the excess-demand function and the total-demand function. See Don Patinkin, Money, Interest, and Prices (Second Edition; New York: Harper and Row, 1965), pp. 3-12.

the deficit, which Poole takes to be the discount rate.[1]

This is the central result of the paper. It is, however, based on a misconception of the choices available to banks. The choice is not between borrowing (or lending) in the interbank market under conditions of uncertainty and borrowing from the Federal Reserve when all the returns are in. That, for example, would imply that banks never use the discount window except on Wednesday afternoons, which certainly is not the case. The choice instead is between the market and the central bank at any moment up to the close of business on the last day. If, at that time, the bank has a reserve shortage, it must face the penalties set by the Federal Reserve. While the nominal "penalties" are tied closely to the discount rate, the true costs of reserve shortages surely are quite a bit higher: observed shortages are extremely rare.[2]

Suppose that both the Federal funds and discount rates are currently 4%. Poole's cost function would suggest that the bank should sell enough reserves to other banks to be sure to attain a deficit by the end of the

---

1. The cost function may be written

$$C = RM_{FF} \int_{\hat{Z}}^{Z_U} E \cdot f(Z) dZ + (RM_{FRB} - RM_{FF}) \int_{Z_L}^{\hat{Z}} B \cdot f(Z) dZ,$$

where RM_{FF} = the Federal funds rate

RM_{FRB} = the discount rate

Z = the unknown change to come in the reserve position between noon and the close of business

E = the magnitude of the excess reserves produced by the stochastic process $f(Z)$

B = the magnitude of borrowing made necessary by the stochastic process

$\hat{Z}$ = the value of Z producing a zero excess position

and Z_L and Z_U are the minimum and maximum values of the function, respectively. The function C is minimized by setting its derivative with respect to funds purchases (FF_p) equal to zero, the E and B variables being functions of FF_p. The two interest rates are assumed to be exogenous to the bank. The solution for the optimum value of FF_p (FF_p^*) is

$$\frac{RM_{FF}}{RM_{FRB}} = P\{[(RES_F)_{noon} + FF_p^* + Z] < 0\},$$

where RES_F = free reserves. It may readily be shown that, since $\hat{Z}$ is a negative function of FF_p, the second-order conditions for a minimum must be met. For a more complete discussion of the cost function, see Poole.

2. See above, p. 18.

day. To derive a cost function more in accord with reality we must replace the discount rate with an estimate of the true penalty--a rate which probably has very little to do with the discount rate itself.

It is unfortunate that the Poole paper reveals so little about the functioning of the Federal funds market, because the approach which he suggests seems to be so promising. Banks do operate in an uncertain world, and it is the stochastic nature of reserve flows which is largely responsible for the market. Professor Poole is the first to develop a model in which this effect becomes explicit; previous models of stochastic reserve flows had abstracted from the funds market.[1] But there are too many problems with Poole's model for it to be of very much help. First, he neglects the possibility of the market being used to conserve resources. Second, he postulates an artificial set of choices available to the individual bank. Third, he assumes a perfectly competitive market, so that the Federal funds rate is taken to be a constant in minimizing the bank's cost function; this rules out the possibility of changing offering rates to increase market activity. And his main policy conclusion, that the discount rate should be pegged at some constant ratio (greater than unity) to the funds rate or the Treasury bill rate, is dependent on the peculiar assumptions of the model and so loses its force.[2]

---

1. See, for example, Daniel Orr and W.G. Mellon, "Stochastic Reserve Losses and Expansion of Bank Credit," American Economic Review, LI (September, 1961), 614-623; and Herschel I. Grossman, "A Stochastic Model of Commercial Bank Behavior," The American Economist, IX (Summer, 1965), 27-34. The first of these papers contains only one footnote about the probability of a role for the funds market (p. 619n), while the second notes that "Space limitations require abstraction from the federal funds market. However, in the course of my work, I have fully investigated the implications of introducing the federal funds market into the model, and have shown that this elaboration does not essentially alter the conclusions presented in this paper," (p. 27). Since his model is built on the assumption that the banking system has no immediate credit items available other than reserves borrowed from the central bank, it seems highly improbable that Grossman's assertion would be valid without the use of some fairly restrictive assumptions about the nature of the market.

2. A number of other writers have made similar recommendations, but their arguments have been based on the desirability of using the discount rate, rather than non-price rationing of credit, as the policy instrument of the discount window, and eliminating the "announcement effects" of changing the discount rate. These arguments are essentially different from Poole's belief that, in an unchanged institutional framework, the pegging operation will stabilize the system's reactions to uncertainty

A Synthesis of Conflicting Concepts

The points which have been made concerning the role of the market now can be briefly summarized.

1. Secular growth in the market since the early Fifties has enabled the banking system to operate with a smaller level of excess reserves, since banks now are able to obtain additional funds when necessary, more cheaply and more quickly than before. This increased efficiency implies that the system will not be able simply to absorb policy actions without passing on the effects to the public. If open market policy is used to contract the reserve base, banks will be less able to draw down their excess reserves, and so will have to contract their portfolio of earning assets. That in turn implies that the Policy action will take hold more quickly and efficiently than it would if the banks were holding a large volume of idle funds.

2. This same effect may have reduced, rather than enhanced, the liquidity of the banking system. Excess reserves are smaller than they once were, and although the funds market may seem like a highly liquid resource for each bank, it may be deceiving for the aggregate system. If the central bank clamps down tightly on reserve availability, so that all banks are short of reserves, the system will be less able than formerly to absorb the squeeze with its excess reserve cushion. This problem reduces the ability of the Federal Reserve to apply restrictive policies without precipitating a liquidity shortage. A given unit of policy input (e.g., a given change in the size of the central bank security portfolio) will bring a greater change in outstanding bank credit. But in an uncertain world the Federal Reserve may be less willing to apply a given magnitude of policy change, for fear that a small error could create a crisis.

3. The short-run effect of the market may be to aid the transmission of policy effects, particularly if policy is being used for expansionary purposes. When the reserve base is expanded through open market purchases, the interbank market may serve to transfer the funds from their point of origin (the central money market) to the banks throughout the country which

---

(p. 784). See the various papers published by the Federal Reserve on their proposed "fundamental reform of the discount mechanism," particularly Priscilla Ormsby, Summary of the Issues Raised at the Academic Seminar on Discounting (Washington: Board of Governors, 1966); and David M. Jones, A Review of the Recent Academic Literature on the Discount Mechanism (Washington: Board of Governors, 1968).

are facing relatively large credit demands. It is sensible to assume that
the initial impact of the expansion may not occur at a critical point,
since the Federal Reserve has little control over the distribution of the
reserves it creates.[1] In that case the new funds might remain idle at
least temporarily, were it not for the existence of an interbank lending
market. In practice, this effect probably would work through a decrease,
not an increase, in trading volume. The normal flow through the market is
toward the money market; large banks acquire funds from the countryside.
When policy is eased, these banks reduce their offering rates on funds,
since they have a more adequate supply of unborrowed reserves. The selling banks then may turn to some other means of investing their own money,
such as making more loans to their own customers.

   4. When policy is tightened, changes in market activity may not be so
favorable. The initial effect of the policy action is felt at the central
money market, as before. But for tightening purposes, this is probably
where the effect should be. When credit demands are excessive, reflecting
an inflationary situation, it is usually the large city banks that contri-
bute most to the problem, since they make the major portion of total loan
volume. If these banks can reduce the pressures on their own portfolios
by buying up reserves from country banks, the economic effects of the
tightening may be reduced. On the other hand, this increased trading
volume may require such a large increase in interest rates that the demand
for credit will slow down enough to bring about the desired cooling of
activity.

   Further discussion on the long-run or secular effects of the funds
market is scarcely needed: everyone is agreed that the market has enabled
banks to reduce idle balances. The real question is whether this fact has
produced a system which is unstable in its reactions to changes in monetary
policy. What happens when the reserve base contracts? The first argument
implies that the banking system will contract asset portfolios in a fashion desired by the central bank. The second argument says that this credit

----

   1. During the early 1920's, open market operations were conducted by
each district Reserve Bank, and so could have been used to affect regional
distribution of funds. More recently, this device has been abandoned in
favor of policy coordination. All transactions in the System Open Market
Account are handled between the Federal Reserve Bank of New York and about
twenty dealers in government securities, most of whom are located in New
York City. See Clark, pp. 161-180.

contraction will be destabilizing to the economy and so will render the
central bank unable or unwilling to act. The final argument is that in
spite of the already reduced volume of excess reserves in the system, the
funds market may still be used to draw in idle funds from around the
country, enabling the city banks to offset the effects of the restrictive
monetary policy.

Surprisingly, there seems to be no problem over the way the market
functions. Trading volume probably will rise when policy is tightened,
and will fall when it is eased.[1] Interest rates will rise or fall correspondingly. What is at issue is the effect that this activity has on
the economy. Those who have written that the market is an aid to policy
transmission believe that the volume changes merely redistribute productive funds or else prevent funds from becoming idle at the wrong time.
The concept of the velocity-increasing offset is that the efficiency of
policy actions is reduced by the act of drawing idle balances into activity.

This discussion has related almost entirely to the enactment of monetary policy through open market operations. In practice the Federal Reserve has a number of tools at its disposal, and the effect of the funds
market may differ, depending on the instrument being used at the time.
Open market operations, by reducing the level of total reserves, can be
offset in only a limited way by increasing sales of those reserves. But
suppose the discount rate is increased in order to restrict the demand for
credit. The funds rate will rise, but the volume of funds being activated
could rise by an even greater proportion, depending on relative elasticities. Thus discount rate changes may be fairly easy to offset. Increases
in reserve requirements would produce the same sort of limitations which
characterize open market operations, while increases in maximum interest
rates payable under Regulation Q would be expected to precipitate reactions
similar to those against the discount rate. That is, policies which
affect the availability of credit directly may be much less subject to
offsetting reactions than will policies which work primarily through the
distribution of assets and the price structure. Methods for testing these
propositions are developed in the next two chapters.

---

1. On the other hand, see Chapter VI below, for evidence to the con-
trary.

Chapter Five. A Theoretical Model of Monetary Policy Transmission

A policy model of an economic system relates changes in variables which are controllable by policy action, designated as instrument variables, to changes in other terms which policy officials wish to influence but cannot affect directly, designated as the targets of policy. Other variables may be introduced as needed to complete the linkage between instrument and target. In his original exposition on this subject, Jan Tinbergen called these "irrelevant" variables.[1] Since his terminology understates the importance of the variables which provide the medium through which policy changes are transmitted to the targets, the term "state" variables will be used here. The model, then, relates changes in the instruments to changes in the targets, using state variables and other data wherever necessary for correct expression of the relationships. Mathematically, this becomes

$$Y = Y(X,Z,W) \tag{11}$$

where Y is a vector of target variables, X a vector of policies, Z a vector of state variables, and W, of other data. This last vector can be ignored for present purposes because it represents data exogenous to the model which, by definition, will not be affected by a policy change. There are I + J + K variables in which we are interested, as follows:

targets: Y_i, $i = 1,\ldots,I$
instruments: X_j, $j = 1,\ldots,J$
state variables: Z_k, $k = 1,\ldots,K$.

The effect of any change in an instrument on any target can be expressed as

$$\frac{dY_i}{dX_j} = \frac{\partial Y_i}{\partial X_j} + \sum_{k=1}^{K} \frac{\partial Y_i}{\partial Z_k} \frac{dZ_k}{dX_j} \tag{12}$$

as long as the instruments have an independent effect on each target.[2]

---

1. On the Theory of Economic Policy (Amsterdam: North Holland, 1952), p. 7. Another term used sometimes is "side-effect variables."

2. For an example of an application of this type of analysis, see Karl A. Fox, Jati K. Sengupta, and Erik Thorbecke, The Theory of Quantitative Economic Policy (Chicago: Rand McNally, 1966), pp. 27-28.

If this condition is violated, equation (12) is still serviceable provided only that the targets Y_m, $m \neq i$ are subsumed under the Z_k. When one
target is isolated for examination, as in equation (12), the other targets
may for that purpose be considered as state variables. What this equation
says is that the effect of a policy change on a target can be divided into
a direct effect and a series of indirect effects operating through all the
other endogenous variables in the model.

The Monetary Policy Mechanism

Instruments. The instruments of monetary policy include open market
operations, discount administration, reserve requirements, and ceiling
rates on time deposits. In addition to these variables which are controlled
directly by the Federal Reserve, there are other instruments which are
monetary by nature, in the sense that they operate on monetary targets
through the monetary sector of the economy, but which are controlled by the
U.S. Treasury. These include the level and composition of Treasury operating balances and the maturity structure of the Federal debt.

Open market operations in government securities, bankers' acceptances,
or other assets directly affect the level of Federal Reserve credit and, as
a residual on the liability side of the central bank balance sheet, total
unborrowed reserves of the member banks. Through reserve requirements
these unborrowed reserves may be divided into those which must be held
against existing deposit liabilities and those which are free to support
additional deposits. That distribution may be treated as a prime factor
affecting the ability of the system to expand its operations. However,
when demands for credit exceed the banks' capabilities under existing reserve levels, the banks may borrow reserves either from each other or from
the central bank. This process may be affected by policy decisions on the
discount rate or on non-price rationing of borrowed reserves.

These "instruments of general monetary control"[1] work through the supply side of bank credit extension. On the demand side, the ceiling rate
on time deposits can be used to alter relative interest rates and hence
the attractiveness of competitive assets. Interest rates paid for time
deposits affect the ability of banks to compete with other financial intermediaries for the public's liquid balances, in turn affecting the level

---

1. See Warren L. Smith, "The Instruments of General Monetary Control,"
National Banking Review, I (September, 1963), 47.

of bank credit. In addition, the maturity structure of the Federal debt
(i.e., debt management policies) can be used to influence the term structure of interest rates and to affect the liquidity of the economy.[1]

Treasury operating balances enter the banking sector insofar as they
are held in the form of deposits at commercial banks. Interpretation of
changes in the level of these government demand deposits depends on whether
one wishes to include them in the money supply.[2] If, for example, changes
in the other instruments are designed to influence some variable such as
currency plus total demand deposits (a variant of the money supply) or
total demand plus time deposits (a variant of the bank credit proxy), then
any shift between government and private deposits will alter the relationship prevailing between the monetary policy action and the final spending
decisions of the public. In that case the Treasury's actions with respect
to its own deposit accounts should properly be regarded as a monetary
policy action. On the other hand, the traditional measures of the money
supply and of bank credit deliberately exclude Treasury deposits, imply-
ing that the general policy instruments are being employed so as to offset
any shift between government and private accounts. If these traditional
measures are indeed being used by the Federal Reserve as indicators, then
we need not be particularly concerned with the level of government deposits.

Targets. The ultimate target of all of this activity is the attain-
ment of the goals set forth in the Employment Act of 1946, namely "maximum
employment, production, and purchasing power."[3] However, monetary

---

1. Debt management is a more complex problem than is implied here,
since it also includes control of the marketability and ownership of the
public debt. The narrower but important problem of controlling the maturity structure of the debt is isolated here in order to limit the size of
the model being developed. For a complete discussion and bibliography of
debt management techniques, see Scott, Government Securities Market. The
effect of changes in the maturity schedule on economic liquidity is discussed in Tilford C. Gaines, Techniques of Treasury Debt Management (New
York: Columbia University and the Free Press, 1962), pp. 239-256. The
relationship to the term structure of interest rates has been widely discussed in the literature; see, for example, Warren L. Smith, Debt Management in the United States: Study Paper No. 19 for the Joint Economic Committee; materials prepared in connection with the Study of Employment,
Growth, and Price Levels (86th Cong., 2nd sess., 1960).

2. This problem is discussed in "The Role of U.S. Government Demand
Deposits in the Monetary Process," Federal Reserve Bank of Cleveland
Economic Review, June, 1969, pp. 2-11.

3. Act of February 20, 1946, 60 Stat. 23; 15 USC 1021. See Board of
Governors, The Federal Reserve System: Purposes and Functions (Fifth
Edition; Washington, 1963), p. 1.

policies influence these targets only through a set of monetary variables
which form the "intermediate targets" of policy. The stability or growth
of these intermediate targets is used as the principal indicator of policy
effects by the central bank and indeed must be the principal target of any
monetary policy action. Failure to attain "maximum employment" can ration-
ally be attributed to, say, fiscal policies; failure to provide for stable
growth in the money supply must be the fault of monetary policies. General
economic conditions dictate the appropriate levels for the intermediate
targets which in turn dictate the appropriate policies to be pursued. In
order to concentrate on the functioning of the monetary sector, the intermediate targets shall here be referred to simply as the targets of monetary
policy.

These intermediate targets fall into three classes: money supply components, credit levels, and long-term interest rates.[1] Furthermore, commercial bank credit may be approximated for both long- and short-term
purposes by the level of total deposits, particularly since this "credit
proxy" is in fact used by the Federal Reserve for that purpose.[2] Three
aggregates--currency, demand deposits, and time deposits held by the non-
bank public--may be combined in various ways to yield each of several different possible targets. Currency plus demand deposits equals the traditionally defined money supply. Adding in time deposits gives the "Fried-
maniac" or broadly defined money supply. Subtracting currency from this
figure yields the bank credit proxy. Thus any model which explains the
influence of changes in policy instruments on each of these three components can be manipulated to determine the effect on any desired combination of terms.

1. Leonall C. Andersen and Jules M. Levine, "A Test of Money Market
Conditions as a Means of Short-Run Monetary Management," National Banking
Review, IV (September, 1966), 42.

2. Board of Governors, Fifty-Third Annual Report (Washington, 1967),
p. 171n. See also James B. Eckert, "The Federal Reserve 'Bank Credit
Proxy'," Banking, LIX (May, 1967), 62-66. The growing use of non-deposit
liabilities since 1968, particularly through the use of the Euro-dollar
market and--most recently--bank-related commercial paper, has led to a pro-
liferation of "adjusted" proxies for total bank credit. See Klopstock for
a discussion of the problem. See Board of Governors, "Monetary Aggregates
and Money Market Conditions in Open Market Policy," Federal Reserve Bulletin, LXII (February, 1971), 91-92, for an illustration of the way the FOMC
uses bank credit proxies.

For most purposes long-term interest rates can be represented either
by the average yield on outstanding government bonds or by the market yield
on top-grade corporate bonds. Either one should affect the cost and hence
the level of investment spending. As Patric H. Hendershott stated the
case in a 1968 paper,

> Recent investigations of the determinants of investment expendi-
> tures indicate that the investment component of final demand is in-
> fluenced significantly by the long-term corporate bond rate and the
> mortgage rate and that it is not much influenced by any other finan-
> cial variables. This suggests that the primary purpose of a finan-
> cial sector of an econometric model is to explain the link between
> monetary policy variables and these two long-term interest rates.[1]

He overstates the situation somewhat, since he ignores the possibility that
some component of total spending other than total aggregate investment
might be influenced by "other financial variables," a possibility con-
firmed by later development of the very "investigations" to which he
refers.[2] Nonetheless, it is clear that long-term interest rates should be
included as a policy target.

State Variables. The state variables of the monetary sector are primarily short-term interest rates and reserve components. The money supply
and bank credit components are influenced, as described above, by the
reserve positions of commercial banks. The positions of member banks are
in turn influenced directly by policy actions and by changes in short-term
interest rates; the member bank positions then exert a strong influence on
the marginal ability of the system to extend credit. Short-term interest
rates are affected by changes in the discount rate and in the rationing of
discount credit, by changes in time-deposit ceilings, and by the debt
management policies of the Treasury. In addition to their influence on
reserve positions, short-term interest rates affect the mix between loans
and secondary reserves in bank portfolios, and they affect long-term
interest rates.

Both the volume of trading and the interest rate in the Federal funds

---

1. "Recent Development of the Financial Sector of Econometric Models,"
Journal of Finance, XXIII (March, 1968), 41-42.

2. The work cited by Hendershott is a series of unpublished papers on
the development of the Federal Reserve--M.I.T. Econometric Model. See
Frank deLeeuw and Edward Gramlich, "The Federal Reserve--M.I.T. Econometric
Model," Federal Reserve Bulletin, LIV (January, 1968), 11-40, and "The
Channels of Monetary Policy," Ibid., LV (June, 1969), 472-491.

market serve as state variables in the transmission of monetary policy to
the intermediate targets. The Federal funds rate is an important short-
term interest rate, since it has an impact on the Treasury bill rate, on
the discount rate (if the Federal Reserve chooses to let it have such an
impact, which it often does), and on the volume of trading in the market.
The latter affects the demand for reserves borrowed at the discount window
and may affect the relationship between the supply of reserves and total
deposits, in the fashion described in Chapter III (pp. 67- 71) as velocity
changes.

Specification of the Model

Now a complete theoretical model of the monetary policy process can be
put together. In order to specify the structure of the financial sector,
it will be necessary to include demand and supply functions for each of
the markets involved in the transmission of policies to the intermediate
targets. Furthermore, these functions must conform to certain balance
sheet constraints linking together many of the variables in the sector.[1]
Beyond that constraint, the arguments of the functions should express
behavioral relationships and should isolate the more important of an
infinite number of underlying causal factors.

Economic theory could be used to support a large number of different
specifications of each function, as can be seen from an examination of the
literature on monetary linkages.[2] Since the purpose of our specifying this
model is to permit the construction of an empirical model to be used to
test hypotheses about the funds market, the choice of variables for

---

1. This point is developed in William C. Brainard and James Tobin,
"Pitfalls in Financial Model Building," American Economic Review, LVIII
(May, 1968), 99-122; and in the work of Carl F. Christ. See, for example,
"A Short-Run Aggregate-Demand Model of the Interdependence and Effects of
Monetary and Fiscal Policies with Keynesian and Classical Interest Elas-
ticities," American Economic Review, LVII (May, 1967), 434-443.

2. Examples of expositions which go beyond the specification of single-
equation or two-equation models are Brainard and Tobin; Hendershott; Lyle
E. Gramley and Samuel B. Chase, Jr., "Time Deposits in Monetary Analysis,"
Federal Reserve Bulletin, LI (October, 1965), 1380-1404; Teigen, "Demand
and Supply Functions for Money in the United States;" Karl Brunner and
Allan H. Meltzer, "Some Further Investigations of Demand and Supply Functions for Money," Journal of Finance, XIX (May, 1964), 240-283; and the
several econometric models of the sector, to which reference is made in
Chapter VI, below (p. 122).

the model will be guided most strongly by the literature on econometric, rather than purely abstract, models.[1] The general form of most of the behavioral relations in the sector is discussed thoroughly in the article by Patric Hendershott mentioned earlier;[2] many of the differences between the model described below and Hendershott's theoretical model either are minor differences in the choice of arguments or are introduced in order to accommodate the role of the Federal funds market.

1. Public demands for demand deposits will be a behavioral function of consumer incomes, business loan demand, and yields on alternative assets. The level of disposable incomes will, if payments habits and interest rates are constant, determine the quantity of current deposits demanded by consumers, since those deposits arise from the process of receiving income and holding it until needed for transactions purposes. As described in Chapter III above (p. 64), there may also be an interest elasticity to the transactions demand for deposits, if consumers (or producers) desire to economize on cash holdings in response to improvements in available yields on highly liquid assets. Those substitute assets might include both Treasury bills and time deposits, so interest rates on both should be included in this function. The demand for business loans also can be included as a prime determinant of business deposit levels, inasmuch as the process of making such loans gives rise to such deposits.

2. The supply of demand deposits is expressed most effectively through a reserve identity.[3] If we focus only on deposits in member banks, this expression is rather simple: the sum of public and government demand deposits must equal required reserves less the portion of those reserves supporting time deposits, divided by the average reserve requirement on demand deposits. Once the average reserve requirements on demand and time deposits and the level of government deposits are given as policy-determined data and the level of time deposits is determined in the manner outlined below, then these equations for the demand and supply of demand deposits

---

1. See Chapter VI, p. 122.

2. Section I (pp. 41-48). These theoretical specifications are similar to much of the earlier study cited above; although Hendershott's empirical estimates are particular to the Federal Reserve--M.I.T. model, his first section is quite general.

3. It is possible to specify a function in which the supply of demand deposits is endogenously determined through an implicit interest rate; this possibility goes beyond the scope of the empirical dimensions of our model. See Gramley and Chase.

will yield the level of publicly held demand deposits and the level of required reserves.

3. The demand for time deposits by the public will be a function of the level of saving and of the yield on time deposits relative to other equally liquid assets. The Treasury bill rate may be able to serve as a proxy for these substitute goods, which would in fact include demand deposits (with an implicit yield) and savings and loan shares.

4. The supply function for time deposits operates through the interest rates offered by banks, on the plausible assumption that banks will supply whatever level is demanded at prevailing rates. This interest rate will be a function of the ceiling rates imposed by the Federal Reserve, plus the degree of pressure put on bank portfolios by the level of credit demands. As the loan-deposit ratio rises (diminishing the banks' cushion of secondary reserves) or the ratio of free to required reserves falls (diminishing the primary reserve cushion), banks should become more willing to offer high rates to attract time deposits.

5. Currency demands will be related to consumer spending and to the implicit yield on demand deposits. Certainly as consumption rises more cash will be needed by the public to handle its transactions. On the other hand, demand deposits will be a good substitute for this additional cash. Any change in the attractiveness of deposits relative to currency should bring a shift in public holdings of the two goods. In the absence of a measurable yield on demand deposits, the level of such deposits could be used here instead, as an ex post proxy.

6. The supply of currency may be taken to be a residual liability of the central bank. The open market operations of the Federal Reserve can be used to determine the value of any single aggregate appearing on the consolidated central bank balance sheet. Depending on the instructions given, this figure--which can be regarded as the instrument of open-market policy-- could be total member bank reserves, total unborrowed reserves, unborrowed reserves plus currency, free reserves, or any one of a very large number of other items or combinations of items. Arguments have been presented for using different figures,[1] and the Reserve System itself is ambiguous

---

1. Hendershott (p. 43), argues for unborrowed reserves by itself, but concedes (p. 46n), that currency could be included. Leonall C. Andersen and Jerry L. Jordan, "Monetary and Fiscal Actions: a Test of Their Relative Importance in Economic Stabilization," Federal Reserve Bank of St. Louis Review, L (November, 1968), 13-14, argue in favor of the "monetary

about exactly what it uses.[1] Nonetheless, if the money supply is one of
the targets of the policy action, then currency levels will have to be
included in the aggregate which is chosen. It will be shown below that
borrowed reserves are probably netted out of the figure. If that point
can be accepted, then the Federal Reserve may be viewed as using the sum of
unborrowed reserves and currency as its open-market policy tool. From
this figure may be subtracted the sums needed for required and free reserves, leaving the quantity of currency supplied. When solved simultaneously with the rest of the model this second reserve identity will com-
bine with public demands for currency to yield outstanding currency and
free reserve levels.

So far, six equations have been outlined for our theoretical model.
They have given us estimates of the three money and credit components com-
prising the first major category of intermediate policy targets. In addition, a number of state variables and policy instruments have been introduced, and consumption, saving, and disposable income have entered as data
exogenous to the monetary sector. Three of the endogenous state variables
have been determined by the equations: free reserves, required reserves,
and interest rates on time deposits. However, other short-term and long-
term rates are still unaccounted for, and the influence of the Federal
funds market has not yet entered the model. The first task, then, is to
account for the level and the term structure of government interest rates.

7. The Treasury bill rate is determined by demands for short-term
government securities, if bills can be used as a proxy for such investments.[2] Bills will be demanded mainly as a secondary bank reserve and as a

---

base," total reserves plus currency. Frank deLeeuw and John Kalchbrenner,
in a comment on the Andersen-Jordan paper, Ibid., LI (April, 1969), 8-9,
argue for unborrowed reserves alone. These alternative specifications are
discussed in James M. Boughton, "Discount Administration in Econometric
Models," Southern Journal of Business, V (July, 1970), 104-114.

1. Board of Governors, The Federal Reserve System: Purposes and Functions, contains only an innocuous reference to "bank reserve positions"
(p. 34). The published records of Open Market Committee policy actions
are more confusing than helpful, since the directives to the account mana-
ger usually are worded in terms of targets rather than instruments.

2. In most econometric studies, this equation is specified with free
reserves on the left side of the equation and with the bill rate as an
argument. The effect of that is that the bill rate is determined in such
models only by commercial bank portfolio pressures. See James M. Boughton,
Eduard H. Brau, Thomas H. Naylor, and William P. Yohe, "A Policy Model of
the United States Monetary Sector," Southern Economic Journal, XXXV (April,

short-term investment by non-bank corporations, both financial and non-financial. The bill rate, therefore, will be functionally related to bank portfolio pressures, to interest rates on alternative uses (and sources, to the extent that bills can be sold by the holder) of funds, and to the relative quantities of securities supplied by the Treasury (i.e., to debt management policies). Perhaps the most important alternative interest rate in this function will be the rate on Federal funds.

8. The long-term government bond rate will be related to the short-term rate via a term-structure hypothesis; furthermore, it will be affected by the same sort of portfolio pressures and debt management practices that affected the bill rate, except now the more long-run aspects of these factors will be decisive.[1] In other words there will be a stable relationship between short- and long-term government interest rates, with deviations from this relationship being generated by changes in the liquidity of the financial community.[2] In this manner demands for government securities of different maturities are determined. If supplies are given by exogenous policy decision, as hypothesized, this process will yield for us the desired interest rates. The supply functions for these securities need not be specified, since they are implied in the above.

The status of the market for business loans is one of the important state variables in the model, since it bears heavily on the portfolio position of the banking system. In particular, increases in business demands for loans relative to total bank deposits will signal a tightening of bank asset positions. Secondary reserves must be reduced to accommodate the increase, and interest costs probably will rise accordingly.

1969), 344. The approach used in the present model has been developed independently in Michael K. Evans, Macroeconomic Activity (New York: Harper & Row, 1969), p. 317.

1. In those models in which the short-term rate is not explicitly determined elsewhere (see note 2, p. 108), it is customary to determine the long-term rate via an equation whose left-hand variable is the difference between the two rates (the term structure) and the arguments of which are similar to those used in our own bond-rate equation. See, for example, Frank deLeeuw, "A Model of Financial Behavior," The Brookings Quarterly Econometric Model of the United States, James Duesenberry, et al. (eds.), (Chicago: Rand McNally, 1965), pp. 464-530.

2. There are a number of theories as to the origin of the term-structure relationship; however, all that is hypothesized here is that some functional relationship will exist between the long and short rates.

9. Demand for business loans may be expressed simply as a function of total business investment spending and of the prevailing interest rates on loans.[1] A more complex rendering of this relationship would include the commercial paper market, the generation of internal funds, or the issuance of new equity as alternatives to bank loans, but adding these probably would not add much for our present purpose.

10. The supply of business credit is controlled through the interest rate. There is probably a good deal of non-price rationing which is not picked up here, and a true supply function would use the full cost of the loans rather than the interest rate. Regardless of which is used for empirical analysis, the cost variable will be determined by the opportunity cost of converting assets into new loans. That cost in turn will depend on yields being obtained on secondary reserve assets, on the portion of total assets already held in loans, and on the ability of the banking system to acquire additional funds. Thus an increase in the Treasury bill rate, for instance, should cause loan rates to rise, since the opportunity cost of acquiring lendable funds has gone up. An increase in the aggregate loan-deposit ratio for the system has the same effect. On the other hand, any increase in the volume of funds moving through the Federal funds market decreases this cost, unless the increase itself requires a large enough increase in the Federal funds and Treasury bill rates to offset the advantage.

So this is where the volume figure comes in. When pressures on the major banks rise, it becomes increasingly difficult for them to obtain the funds they need to satisfy the credit demands which they face. In order to ration their resources, they may be expected to increase their lending charges. At the same time, they will be making a vigorous effort to obtain additional resources to lend at these rising rates. By increasing offering rates for Federal funds money-market banks can draw in a larger volume of such funds from around the country. The fact of the rate increase causes lending costs to rise, but the volume increase taken by itself works in the opposite direction.

One note of explanation may be in order here. The above exposition of the credit supply function has implied that credit demands and portfolio

---

1. The structure of the commercial loan market used here is derived substantially from Stephen M. Goldfeld, Commercial Bank Behavior and Economic Activity (Amsterdam: North-Holland, 1966), pp. 62-68 and pp. 82-88. See also Hendershott, p. 46.

pressures will be centered in a fairly small group of banks. In order for
the banking system to be able to operate with the flexibility assumed in
this process, there must be a very large number of banks not subject to
these same pressures. Some evidence in support of this view is given in a
recent Federal Reserve publication on the role played by a very few banks
in New York City:

> A lion's share of the pressure on the banking system resulting
> from the combination of excessive credit demands and monetary re-
> straint during 1966 fell on the eight large money market banks in
> New York City. Over the post-World War II period, the role of the
> New York City banks as a major supplier of business credit had hardly
> diminished, despite the more rapid growth of many regions outside the
> industrial northeast and mid-Atlantic states. In 1966, the large
> New York City banks held about 29 percent of total business loans
> outstanding at all member banks, only a slightly lesser share than
> the 31 percent in 1946.[2]

The extreme concentration existing in this industry is beyond dispute.

This leaves us with only the Federal funds market to specify for the
theoretical model of the sector to be complete.

11. The demand for Federal funds is manifested primarily through the
interest rate, since it is a buyer's market. It has been shown at several
points in this discussion that increases in credit demands, portfolio pressures, or borrowing costs in alternative markets will lead the major borrowers of Federal funds to increase their offering rates. Hence a tightening of reserve positions at major banks, an increase in business loan
rates, or an increase in the discount rate should bring about a Federal
funds rate increase, representing increased demand for such funds. A rise
in the Treasury bill rate would bring the same sort of change, but this
relationship has already been included in the demand function for Treasury
bills.

12. The supply of funds into the market will be functionally related
to free reserve levels at those banks which face relatively light credit
demands and to the difference between the funds rate and the bill rate.
That is, two conditions must be met before a bank will sell Federal funds.
First, it must have funds to sell. Second, the sale of the funds in the
Federal funds market must be more attractive than alternative uses of the
money, such as buying Treasury bills.

----

1. Dolores P. Lynn, Reserve Adjustments of the Eight Major New York
City Banks During 1966 (Washington: Board of Governors, 1968), p. 7.

At this juncture an assumption implicit in the entire specification of the theoretical model must be made explicit. This assumption is the validity of the Federal Reserve view that reserves borrowed from the discount department will not effectively be used to support growth in bank credit. This view, unfortunately, is not unambiguous. The foreword to Regulation A states that "such borrowing adds to the supply of reserves of the banking system as a whole" and "has an important bearing on the effectiveness of System credit policy."[1] If that were their true concern, however, they could very easily offset any increase in borrowed reserves with a corresponding decrease in unborrowed reserves. Instead they apparently choose to regard borrowed reserves as a different sort of animal. Rather than being a continuous source of funds to banks as an alternative to unborrowed reserves, the discount window is administered so as to provide temporary and emergency funds, with specific instructions that the borrowing bank is to use the funds only to permit it to reduce its loan portfolio more slowly than it otherwise would be forced to do. "Under ordinary conditions, the continuous use of Federal Reserve credit by a member bank over a considerable period of time is not regarded as appropriate."[2] But what does this mean? Certainly any increase in the aggregate volume of borrowing is capable of generating additional credit. The point which the Board of Governors seems to be making is that we need not be concerned about this increase as long as the fact of the increased borrowing places enough pressure on the member banks to reduce credit in the very near future.

If this representation of the situation is valid, then reserves obtained from the discount window may be viewed as a qualitatively different asset to the banks from reserves obtained in any other way. Yet the description of the market for borrowed reserves presented in Part One of this work started with the assumption that reserves from the discount window would be perfectly substitutable for Federal funds borrowed by a bank, since each would have the same effect on the bank's balance sheet. For both of these propositions to be valid, must it also be true that borrowed

---

1. Board of Governors, Regulation A: Advances and Discounts by Member Banks, 12 CFR 201.0, revised effective February 15, 1955.

2. Ibid. At the present time, the Federal Reserve System is undertaking a major study aimed at reform of the discount window. See Board of Governors, Reappraisal of the Federal Reserve Discount Mechanism: Report of a System Committee, and associated papers; also Joint Economic Committee, U.S. Congress, Federal Reserve Discount Mechanism: Hearings (90th Cong., 2d sess., September 11 and 17, 1968).

Federal funds will not be used over time to support credit expansion? That would nullify the importance of the market. The resolution of this apparent paradox is obtained through a close look at its time dimension. At the time a bank borrows reserve funds, it may regard the discount window and the interbank market as perfect substitutes. To do so, however, it must take into consideration the full cost of the funds to be borrowed from the Federal Reserve, and this cost will include the necessity of having to re-pay the loan in a short period of time. If credit pressures persist, this cost will rise. The Federal funds rate, keeping pace with the full cost of discounting, will rise above the discount rate itself. The effect on the banking system will be that the discounted funds will be less effective for credit expansion than the funds obtained through the interbank market.

This dichotomy implies that the volume of borrowed reserves need not appear in our theoretical model. As was stated above, the Federal Reserve's open market operations may be undertaken so as to specify a desired level of unborrowed reserves plus currency. That decision itself implies that the Federal Reserve is not concerned with the level of borrowed reserves, as long as they have adequate control over the cost of those reserves. If we further assume that this control is indeed adequate, so that borrowed reserves will have little or no impact on aggregate credit expansion, then the magnitude of that figure will be of no interest to us. Whether this is a valid representation of the process is an empirical question, one which has not adequately been tested in the literature.[1]

That leaves the model with twelve structural relationships defining all the necessary linkages between Federal Reserve and other monetary policies and the intermediate or monetary targets of those policies. The variables which have been used are as follows:[2]

Policy Instruments:

BF_S short-term government debt
BF_L long-term government debt
BF_{PUB} total government debt
DD_{GF} government demand deposits
RES_{NBC} unborrowed reserves plus currency

1. See Boughton, "Discount Administration in Econometric Models."

2. This notation is derived from Boughton, Brau, Naylor and Yohe. For more detailed explanations of the variables, see Appendix A, below.

RM_{FRB} discount rate

RM_{TDM} ceiling rate on time deposits

RRR_{DD} reserve requirement on demand deposits

RRR_{TD} reserve requirement on time deposits

Targets:

CURR   currency

DD   demand deposits

TD   time deposits

RM_{GL} interest rate on government bonds

State Variables:

CL   commercial (business) loans

FF   volume of Federal funds trading

RES_F free reserves

RES_R required reserves

RM_{CL} interest rate on commercial loans

RM_{FF} interest rate on Federal funds

RM_{GS} interest rate on Treasury bills

RM_{TD} interest rate on time deposits

Exogenous Data:

C   consumption

S   saving

I   investment

Y_D disposable income.

There are twelve endogenous variables, four of which are policy targets. They are related to the thirteen exogenous variables by the twelve functions specified verbally above and mathematically below. In the equations listed here, the * indicates the determination of a desired value.

A. Demand Deposits:

Public demands for demand deposits:

$$DD^* = f_1(Y_D, CL, RM_{GS}, RM_{TD}) \tag{13}$$

Member-bank supply of demand deposits:

$$DD + DD_{GF} \equiv \frac{RES_R - RRR_{TD} \cdot TD}{RRR_{DD}} \tag{14}$$

B. Time Deposits:

Public demands for time deposits:

$$TD^* = f_3(S, RM_{TD}, RM_{GS}) \tag{15}$$

Member-bank supply of time deposits:

$$RM_{TD}^* = f_4(RM_{TDM}, \frac{CL}{DD+TD}, \frac{RES_F}{RES_R}) \tag{16}$$

C. Currency:

Public demands for currency:

$$CURR^* = f_5(C, DD) \tag{17}$$

Currency supplied through the banking system:

$$CURR \equiv RES_{NBC} - RES_R - RES_F \tag{18}$$

D. Government Securities:

Demand for Treasury bills:

$$RM_{GS}^* = f_7(\frac{RES_F}{RES_R}, RM_{FF}, RM_{FRB}, \frac{BF_S}{BF_{PUB}}) \tag{19}$$

Demand for Treasury bonds:

$$RM_{GL}^* = f_8(\frac{CL}{DD+TD}, RM_{GS}, \frac{BF_L}{BF_{PUB}}) \tag{20}$$

E. Business Loans

Public demand for business loans:

$$CL^* = f_9(I, RM_{CL}) \tag{21}$$

Bank supply of business loans:

$$RM_{CL}^* = f_{10}(RM_{GS}, \frac{CL}{DD+TD}, FF) \tag{22}$$

F. Federal Funds

Demand for Federal funds:

$$RM_{FF}^* = f_{11}(\frac{RES_F}{RES_R}, RM_{CL}, RM_{FRB}) \tag{23}$$

Supply of Federal funds:

$$FF^* = f_{12}(RES_F, RM_{FF}, RM_{GS}) \tag{24}$$

Uses of the Model

The purpose of specifying a complete model of the financial sector is to enable us to go beyond a static look at the derivatives, multipliers, or elasticities of single functions. In the model just specified, the funds market performs multiple roles. The signs of the coefficients are easily predicted, since they result directly from the analysis presented in Part One. But the net effects on the process of policy transmission over any length of time are not so easily seen. Before that task can be approached, we first need to derive the hypotheses to be tested.

What is really at issue here is the effect of Federal funds activity on the efficacy of monetary policy, which may be defined as the absolute value of each dY/dX term. Recalling equation (12),

$$\frac{dY_i}{dX_j} = \frac{\partial Y_i}{\partial X_j} + \sum_{k=1}^{K} \frac{\partial Y_i}{\partial Z_k} \frac{dZ_k}{dX_j} \ , \tag{12}$$

there are two state variables in which we are interested, FF and RM_{FF}. Labeling these Z_1 and Z_2, the various effects of policy actions can be re-written as

$$\frac{dY_i}{dX_j} = \frac{\partial Y_i}{\partial X_j} + \frac{\partial Y_i}{\partial Z_1} \frac{dZ_1}{dX_j} + \frac{\partial Y_i}{\partial Z_2} \frac{dZ_2}{dX_j} + \sum_{k=3}^{K} \frac{\partial Y_i}{\partial Z_k} \frac{dZ_k}{dX_j} \tag{25}$$

or, lumping together all the partial effects operating through the other endogenous variables into the "direct" effect,

$$\frac{dY_i}{dX_j} = \frac{\partial Y_i}{\partial Z_1} \frac{dZ_1}{dX_j} + \frac{\partial Y_i}{\partial Z_2} \frac{dZ_2}{dX_j} + \frac{\hat{\partial Y_i}}{\hat{\partial X_j}} \ . \tag{26}$$

This last equation divides the total effect of a change in a policy instrument on a target into three components: the part due to induced changes in the volume of trading in Federal funds, the part due to induced changes in the interest rate on funds, and the part due to everything else. Furthermore, each of the first two parts is divided into the effect of the policy change on the Federal funds variable and the effect of that change on the target. Our goal now is the measurement of each of these terms.

Before proceeding, we must assign some time dimension to the model. The ultimate effect of the market on policy efficacy may be quite different from its initial impact. On the other hand, an effect felt three years after the policy change is initiated must be considered to be different from an effect felt immediately. Both of these factors can be accounted for by measuring both the policy change and the target change in present values over some length of time. Starting with a control solution to the model, the level of an instrument may be altered for an arbitrarily

selected period, and a present value of the magnitude of this exogenous
shock may be measured. Then, over the same length of time, the change in
the present value of the target variable is computed, and the ratio of
this value to the instrument change can be interpreted as a measure of the
efficacy of policy under the specified conditions.[1]

To isolate from this figure the effect of activity in the Federal funds
market, the model has to be modified. For example, the effect of Federal
funds trading volume on the entire set of endogenous variables in the model
may be eliminated by respecifying equation (22) so as to drop FF. If, in
addition, equation (19) is respecified without RM_{FF}, the whole market is
effectively isolated from the rest of the model. Certainly we would have
to be extremely cautious in deriving empirical estimates of the modified
model, because the remaining parameters may not remain stable. That is,
if the other coefficients simply absorb the effects eliminated, so that
some other variable serves as a proxy for the ones removed, nothing would
be gained by the process. At least in theory, though, the modifications
may be made. Then any remaining value for each dY/dX would have to be due
to forces other than the eliminated factors. The difference between the
original and the modified estimates would be the effect of the funds market on policy transmission.

Summary

This chapter has presented a formal model of the way the Federal funds
market affects the rest of the monetary sector of the economy, with
emphasis on its role in the transmission of monetary policies. Each of the
relationships described in previous chapters is included in the model: the
possibility of trading volume being used to increase aggregate credit extension is there, along with the cost and distribution effects of changes
in prevailing interest rates. The model is designed to be used to test
hypotheses about the net effect of the market on the efficacy of policy
actions. There are X policy instruments and Y targets, so that the model
contains X·Y policy multipliers. It is quite possible that the effects of

---

1. This method is arbitrary, and serves only to develop summary
measures for different types of policies. For an analogous solution to a
related problem, see Gary Fromm and Paul Taubman, Policy Simulations with
an Econometric Model (Washington: Brookings, 1968), 84-85.

the market on the various multipliers will not be uniform. That will not prevent us, however, from at least revealing this diversity and specifying the conditions under which different effects may be expected.

Chapter Six. An Econometric Test

The hypothesis which we now shall attempt to refute through empirical testing is that the Federal funds market does not function so as to provide a significant offset to the efficacy of monetary policy. Mathematically, our null hypothesis is that the full derivatives of the monetary targets with respect to the policy instruments are not diminished by the effects of the partial derivatives related to the variables of the Federal funds market.[1] The dimensions of these derivatives were set forth in Chapter V, and they will be given empirical content momentarily.

The first section of this chapter deals with the methodological problems inherent in the empirical derivation of complex elasticities and multipliers. Then the theoretical model of the previous chapter is presented again, with the parameters of the model made explicit through empirical estimation. The remainder of the chapter is devoted to the validation and detailed analysis of the properties of the complete model.

Methodology

A complete empirical test of the role of the Federal funds market in transmitting monetary policy actions would require a model of the process under each of several institutional frameworks. The monetary system of the United States is nonlinear by nature, and it is subject to structural shifts which may alter substantially the relationships among the variables which comprise the system. One example of a nonlinearity in the sector is the action of the loan-deposit or the loan-asset ratios of the banking system; these ratios act as a capacity index, so that banks become less

---

1. Recalling equation (26), p. 116, this hypothesis is equivalent to
$$H_0 \Rightarrow \frac{dY_i}{dX_j} - \frac{\partial Y_i}{\partial X_j} \geq 0.$$

willing to expand loans at given rates as the portion of their portfolio
already in loans increases. Another example is the well-known asymmetry
of monetary policy effects: a tightening of policy is more binding on
the banks than is an easing. A good example of a structural shift in the
sector is the Federal funds market itself. Another might be the growth of
the Euro-dollar market, which could be a significant factor determining the
effect of the funds market. Obviously the construction of a model of sufficient generality to offset the localizing effect of nonlinearities and to
cover every structural shift would be beyond the scope of the present work.
It may, however, be possible to develop a model covering a specific period
of time and to extrapolate more general conclusions from it. That will be
the goal of this chapter.

The technical limitation produced by the existence of nonlinearities
is that there are no general multipliers in such a model. In a linear
system one can calculate the impact that a change in an exogenous term will
have on any endogenous variable, knowing that the effect will hold regardless of initial conditions. In a nonlinear system only "local" effects--
multipliers for the particular circumstances assumed--can be calculated.[1]

As set forth in Chapter V, the purpose of constructing a model of the
policy transmission process is to enable us to calculate the effects of
changes in various monetary policies and to isolate the effects which are
attributable to activity in the Federal funds market. Essentially these
effects have two parts: the transmission of a policy change from an instrument variable to the relevant variable in the funds market and the
further transmission of the effect to the target variable. Ignoring
secondary impacts for the moment (i.e., changes which operate through two
or more endogenous variables before reaching the target), and recalling the
notation employed in Chapter V, the impact of the funds market may be
summarized as

$$\frac{\partial Y_i}{\partial Z_1} \frac{\partial Z_1}{\partial X_j} + \frac{\partial Y_i}{\partial Z_2} \frac{\partial Z_2}{\partial X_j}.$$

In this simplified situation our task would be to measure these four partial derivatives as accurately as possible. If there were indeed no
secondary or higher-order policy effects and if the system were completely

---

1. Fox, Sengupta, and Thorbecke, p. 28.

linear and recursive so that problems of simultaneous determination could
be ignored, then these values could be read directly from the parameters
of the model. Unfortunately the model, in order to be realistic, must be
more complex. The simple partial derivatives will be replaced by poly-
nomial expressions that are interdependent and are not directly extractable
from the model. In general each of the above terms will be replaced by an
expression of the form

$$\frac{\partial Y_i}{\partial Z_k} \frac{dZ_k}{dX_j} \,, \quad k = 1,\, 2.$$

The derivatives of the Z_k with respect to the instruments will be observable in the reduced form of the model; however the linkages between the
funds market and the targets will be obscured by the fact of their simultaneity. Both variables are determined simultaneously within the model, so
that the impact of one upon the other cannot be isolated.[1] In the nonlinear simultaneous system, neither can the effects of the two Federal
funds parameters (the interest rate and the volume of transactions) be
isolated completely from each other. When the above derivatives are expanded to reveal the full set of linkages in the model, it becomes apparent
that some of those linkages operate through both of the Federal funds variables at the same time, causing an overlap from which the desired information cannot be extracted.

There are at least two ways to cope with these difficulties. One would
be to ignore the nonlinearities and simultaneous relationships in the system and calculate a linear recursive model. This would be a highly desirable approach if one could work with a short enough data interval, say a
week in length. That would not only justify a recursive structure, it
would also permit abstraction from capacity limitations, the principal
source of nonlinearity, by making possible a very short-run analysis. At
the present time, however, data of good quality do not exist for a number
of important variables over intervals of less than three months. This
limitation applies particularly to the components of aggregate demand and
to interest rates on time deposits.

A second approach, which is adopted here, is to use computer simulations

---

1. A good introduction to the use of reduced-form analysis may be
found in Arthur S. Goldberger, Impact Multipliers and Dynamic Properties
of the Klein-Goldberger Model (Amsterdam: North-Holland, 1959).

under alternative specifications of a model in order to isolate information which hopefully will correspond to the unobservable data described
above. The particular simulations to be run will be described below. For
the moment two observations are in order. First, the data generated by
computer simulations are not essentially different from those which could
be produced under a detailed analysis of the reduced form parameters of the
model;[1] the choice of this method of data generation is dictated solely by
its comparative ease of computation and digestion. Second, one must keep
in mind while analyzing the simulation output that an attempt is being made
to create artificially an environment from which information can be re-
trieved; precise results cannot be expected.

Estimation of an Empirical Model

Before the simulation study can proceed, a working empirical model of
the monetary system must be specified. At the time that work on this model
was initiated (September, 1967), there were three major published models on
which to build.[2] Since that time, three additional models, including an
earlier version of the present model, have appeared.[3] None of these pre-
decessors, except for the last, incorporated any of the variables of the
Federal funds market;[4] therefore they are of use only as guides for the
specification of relationships.

The theoretical form of the present model was specified in Chapter V
and will not be repeated here. Most of the problems involved in deriving

1. Although nonlinear models do not have an exactly corresponding reduced form, one can be approximated through linearization. See Goldberger,
pp. 14-20.

2. DeLeeuw, "A Model of Financial Behavior;" Goldfeld; and Teigen,
"An Aggregated Quarterly Model of the U.S. Monetary Sector, 1953-1964."

3. DeLeeuw and Gramlich; Michael K. Evans and Lawrence R. Klein, The
Wharton Econometric Forecasting Model (2nd Edition; Philadelphia: University of Pennsylvania, 1968); and Boughton, Brau, Naylor, and Yohe.

4. A recent paper contains a reduced-form equation illustrating the
influence of certain institutional phenomena on the Federal funds rate.
See Robert B. Platt, "The Interest Rate on Federal Funds: an Empirical
Approach," Journal of Finance, XXV (June, 1970), 585-597. A Federal Re-
serve Board project to estimate a monthly model of the financial system
also examines the parameters of the funds market; Robert T. Parry, James L.
Pierce, and Thomas D. Thomson, "Project Report on the Monthly Money Market
Model," unpublished, 1968.

empirical estimates of the functions are discussed in the April, 1969
article by Boughton, Brau, Naylor, and Yohe. All that is necessary here is
to present the regression results and to comment on their quality and on
the compromises which some of them represent.

The regressions were estimated by two-stage least squares,[1] using unadjusted quarterly data. As listed below, the coefficients are accompanied
wherever appropriate by their standard errors in parentheses. The coefficient of determination, adjusted for equational degrees of freedom ($\bar{R}^2$),
the Durbin-Watson autocorrelation coefficient (DW), and the standard error
of the equation estimate (SE) are given for each regression. The period
(in quarters) over which each regression was estimated is also listed.

The Complete Model

A. Demand Deposits

Public demands for demand deposits:

$$\Delta DD = -1.56 - \underset{(.02)}{0.04}\ DD_{-1} - \underset{(.0028)}{0.0037}\ RM_{TD} \cdot W \tag{27}$$

$$-\underset{(.0012)}{0.0066}\ RM_{GS} \cdot W + \underset{(.12)}{0.35}\ \Delta CL + \underset{(.03)}{0.09}\ Y_D$$

$$+ .36Q_1 - 1.84Q_2 - .08Q_3 + 1.56Q_4$$

$\bar{R}^2 = .87$

DW $= 1.38$

SE $= 0.59$ (1951 I - 1966 IV)

Member-bank supply of demand deposits:

$$DD + DD_{GF} \equiv \frac{RES_R - RRR_{TD} \cdot TD}{RRR_{DD}} \tag{28}$$

---

1. The computer program used for the regressions is described in
Appendix B.

B. Time Deposits

Public demands for time deposits:

$$\Delta TD = -0.89 + 0.001 \underset{(.021)}{TD_{-1}} + 0.014 \underset{(.003)}{RM_{TD}} \cdot W \tag{29}$$

$$-0.01 \underset{(.001)}{RM_{GS}} \cdot W + 0.07 \underset{(.036)}{S_{-1}} + .30Q_1$$

$$+ .29Q_2 - .04Q_3 - .55Q_4$$

$\overline{R}^2 = .74$

DW = 1.23

SE = 0.71   (1951 I - 1966 IV)

Member-bank supply of time deposits:

$$\Delta RM_{TD} = -0.13 - 0.0043 \underset{(.0047)}{RM_{TD_{-1}}} + 0.27 \underset{(.02)}{\Delta RM_{TDM}} \tag{30}$$
$$\phantom{\Delta RM_{TD} = }\underset{(.05)}{}$$

$$+ 0.89 \underset{(.26)}{CL/(DD+TD)}$$

$\overline{R}^2 = .73$

DW = 2.05

SE = 0.03   (1951 I - 1966 IV)

C. Currency

Public demands for currency:

$$\Delta CURR = -0.05 + 0.07 \underset{(.02)}{CURR_{-1}} - 0.02 \underset{(.006)}{DD} \tag{31}$$

$$+ 0.03 \underset{(.014)}{\Delta C} - .22Q_1 - .01Q_2$$

$$+ .28Q_3 - .05Q_4$$

$\overline{R}^2 = .74$

DW = 1.06

SE = 0.19   (1951 I-1966 IV)

Currency supplied through the banking system:

$$CURR \equiv RES_{NBC} - RES_R - RES_F \tag{32}$$

D. Government Securities

Demand for Treasury bills:

$$\Delta RM_{GS} = 0.19 - 0.54\ RM_{GS_{-1}} + 0.47\ RM_{FF} \quad\quad (33)$$
$$\phantom{\Delta RM_{GS} = }(.08)\quad (.11)\quad\quad\ (.10)$$

$$+\ 0.41\ \Delta RM_{FRB} - 22.14\ \Delta(RES_F/RES_{NBC})$$
$$(.16)\quad\quad\ (12.40)$$

$$+\ 8.46\ \Delta(BF_S/BF_{PUB})$$
$$(2.76)$$

$\bar{R}^2 = .82$

DW = 1.48

SE = 0.17   (1954 III - 1966 IV)

Demand for Treasury bonds:

$$\Delta RM_{GL} = -\ 0.22 - 0.04\ RM_{GL_{-1}} + 0.25\ \Delta RM_{GS}$$
$$\phantom{\Delta RM_{GL} = -\ 0.22}(.02)\quad\quad\quad (.036)$$

$$+\ 1.87\ CL/(DD+TD) - 1.15\ \Delta(BF_L/BF_{PUB}) \quad\quad (34)$$
$$(.85)\quad\quad\quad\quad\quad (.87)$$

$$+\ .02Q_1 + .02Q_2 + .02Q_3 - .06Q_4$$

$\bar{R}^2 = .52$

DW = 2.23

SE = 0.09   (1951 I - 1966 IV)

E. Business Loans

Public demand for business loans:

$$\Delta CL = -\ 0.48 + 0.15\ CL_{-1} - 0.01\ RM_{CL}\cdot W \quad\quad (35)$$
$$(.06)\quad\quad (.003)$$

$$+\ 0.22\ I - .41Q_1 + .13Q_2 - .20Q_3$$
$$(.08)$$

$$+\ .48Q_4$$

$\bar{R}^2 = .71$

DW = 1.97

SE = 0.45   (1960 I - 1966 IV)

Bank supply of business loans:

$$\Delta RM_{CL} = -\underset{(.32)}{1.04} - \underset{(.098)}{0.096}\, RM_{CL-1} + \underset{(.09)}{0.16}\, \Delta RM_{GS} \tag{36}$$

$$+ \underset{(.14)}{0.25}\, \Delta RM_{FRB} + \underset{(2.3)}{7.7}\, CL/(DD{+}TD)$$

$$\underset{(2.3)}{-7.7}\, FF/(DD{+}TD)$$

$\bar{R}^2 = .56$

$DW = 1.99$

$SE = 0.10$ $\qquad$ (1960 I - 1966 IV)

F. Federal Funds

Demand for Federal funds:

$$\Delta RM_{FF} = -\underset{(.27)}{0.68} - \underset{(.05)}{0.04}\, RM_{FF-1} - \underset{(11.61)}{46.35}\, \Delta(RES_F/RES_{NBC}) \tag{37}$$

$$+ \underset{(.07)}{0.17}\, RM_{CL} + \underset{(.14)}{0.84}\, \Delta RM_{FRB}$$

$\bar{R}^2 = .80$

$DW = 1.72$

$SE = 0.18$ $\qquad$ (1954 IV - 1966 IV)

Supply of Federal funds:

$$\Delta FF = -\underset{(.17)}{0.71} - \underset{(.14)}{0.83}\, FF_{-1} + \underset{(.001)}{0.007}\, RM_{FF}{\cdot}RES_{NBC} \tag{38}$$

$$+ \underset{(.20)}{0.96}\, RES_F$$

$\bar{R}^2 = .59$

$DW = 1.72$

$SE = 0.11$ $\qquad$ (1960 I - 1966 IV)

The notation is the same as that employed in Chapter V, with the following additions:

W   Public wealth

Q_i Quarterly dummies for seasonal adjustment

The precise definitions of each variable and the data sources are listed in Appendix A.

The general form of the model may be seen by inspection of the demand deposit regression as a typical equation. The theoretical sepcification (from p. 114) was

$$DD^* = f_1 (RM_{TD}, RM_{GS}, CL, Y_D) \tag{13}$$

For empirical estimation, three aspects of the relation had to be added. First, a stock-adjustment framework was introduced by including the lagged value of the left-hand variable. Second, seasonal factors were introduced, since unadjusted data were being used. Third, the interest rates were multiplied by the level of public wealth in order to make the equation homogeneous of degree zero in dollar values.[1] This same pattern was employed consistently throughout the model, except in those cases in which the seasonal factors were not statistically significant.

The only other modification in the demand deposit equation is that commercial loans enter in first-difference, rather than level, form. This change was necessitated by the multicollinearity introduced by the level of CL. Using the latter results in a very small coefficient half the size of its standard error; the coefficient on RM_{TD} is also adversely affected in that case. Converting to ΔCL introduces no serious conceptual difficulties.

A slight degree of autocorrelation is present in the demand deposit regression but not enough to be troublesome. The Durbin-Watson statistic serves only as a rough guide here, since it is known to be biased when lagged endogenous variables are present.[2]

---

1. Derivations for these concepts are discussed in Boughton, Brau, Naylor, and Yohe.

2. M. Nerlove and K.F. Wallis, "Use of the Durbin-Watson Statistic in Inappropriate Situations," Econometrica, XXXIV (January, 1966), 235-238.

The time deposit block exhibits no real problems except for the unproductive results on the stock-adjustment variables. In both the supply and the demand equations, coefficients essentially equal to zero are obtained. A literal interpretation of this result would be that a lag of nearly infinite length would be required for time deposits to adjust to desired levels. Explanations for this problem have been discussed elsewhere;[1] the importance of the subject for this chapter's work is that the time required for the system to react to exogenous shocks is lengthened considerably. In essence the model takes on a very strong autoregressive character and requires a greater force to move the system from its normal path.

The currency equation suffers from both autocorrelation and an unsatisfactory stock-adjustment coefficient. However, a number of alternative specifications of the relation were attempted without any net gain.

The bill rate equation (33), one of the most important relations in the model, is also one of the most satisfying. An excellent fit has been obtained and no serious problems are observable. Similar enthusiasm may be expressed for the long-term rate equation, except that the statistical fit is not so good.

A good relation is obtained for the loan demand function, except that the recurring problem of the lagged dependent variable crops up again. The supply function requires some additional comment. When the function is fitted in theoretical form, coefficients not significantly different from zero are obtained for the FF variable, regardless of the form in which the regression is specified. The original purpose of the equation was to estimate the relationship prevailing between the volume of funds trading and the volume of commercial loans, to determine the extent to which funds trading permitted banks to expand loans. Upon completion of the regression runs, it became clear that a very serious simultaneity problem existed. Apparently the causal linkage from FF to loan volume was either small enough or indirect enough to be offset in statistical testing by an effect in the opposite direction by which, for example, an increase in loans might be made possible by a corresponding reduction in sales of Federal funds rather than an increase in purchases. One could conclude from this evidence that the funds market does not serve to support lending activity. However, the evidence is rather weak in light of the small number of observations (28) available for this particular relation. It is quite possible

---

1.   Boughton, Brau, Naylor, and Yohe, pp. 339-340.

that this fact, along with the inherent difficulties in specifying the precise link between the two volume figures in a highly aggregated system, is obscuring the relationship that we are attempting to measure. It would seem appropriate to reserve judgment on the issue temporarily.

The hypotheses summarized at the end of Chapter IV depend for their resolution on the effect of trading volume on bank loans. If the impact is either zero or negative, then clearly the banking system will be unable to offset policy changes by attracting larger or smaller quantities of reserve funds into the market. If the impact is positive and large, then it may be possible for the banks to offset any reserve contractions by increases in velocity, and conversely. It already has been noted that the data presently available reveal an effect that is approximately zero. The next step, to account for the possibility that the data limitations have led to a spurious result, is to force a positive coeffficient on FF and then determine through simulation of the complete system whether a significant offset occurs. This step will provide the most favorable conditions possible for finding a policy offset, in the hope that some definitive conclusions will thereby be made possible.

The supply equation actually used (equation 36) uses a coefficient of unity, as can be seen by solving the equation for CL:

$$CL = 0.134 \ (DD+TD) + (.130 \ \Delta RM_{CL} - .021 \ \Delta RM_{GS} - .033 \ \Delta RM_{FRB}) \cdot (DD+TD) + FF.$$

This function implies that every dollar of reserve funds that enters the funds market immediately increases business loan volume by an equivalent amount. Each dollar represents a shift of idle balances into productive activity. Thus the model clearly poses the supreme test against the hypothesis that volume changes will not offset monetary policy.

The last two equations of the model deal with the Federal funds market. The only difference between the theoretical and the empirical versions of these functions is that the Treasury bill rate has been dropped from the supply function because of its lack of explanatory power. Otherwise there seem to be no problems in the estimation of the relationships in this market. Note the very strong responses to changes in free reserves. The supply of funds moves almost dollar-for-dollar with free reserves, and the interest rate reacts inversely, as expected. It is also interesting to compare the autoregressive character of the quarterly interest rate series with the virtually independent series of observations on the volume figures. This pattern, of course, is highly visible in the original data series.

Validation

The question of whether the model is a valid representation of the true economic system involves some rather complex issues and therefore yields only imcomplete answers. To the extent that the model has been developed carefully from sound economic theories, as Chapter V attempted to demonstrate, it should be a valid model of the real world. However, the theory could be invalid, the functional form could be misspecified, and the data could contain errors of various sorts. Thus the only way that the model can be tested for validity is for its properties to be tested against the historical behavior of the real world. A number of tests of this type could be made. The two most common are the generation of simulated values for the endogenous variables over the period for which the model was estimated, in order to compare these values with the historical values; and the generation of forecasts of values for the endogenous variables on dates outside of the estimation period, again to compare these simulated values with the observed series. Both types of tests have been made for this model and are reported below.

Once the values have been generated for the relevant variables, some sort of statistical test is necessary in order to compare the simulated and the historical values. A number of such tests exist[1] and have been applied to models similar to the present one.[2] Some recent testing has been done on this model by Vincent J. Geraci at Duke University.[3] Geraci has applied stochastic simulations to a version of the model which includes the complete variance-covariance matrix. His tests permit the computation of a variance band around the simulated time paths, which then can be compared with the historical series to determine whether the hypothesis that

---

1. See, for example, Thomas H. Naylor and J.M. Finger, "Verification of Computer Simulation Models," Management Science, XIV (October, 1967), B92-B101.

2. For example, Thomas H. Naylor, William H. Wallace, and W. Earl Sasser, "A Computer Simulation Model of the Textile Industry," Journal of the American Statistical Association, LXII (December, 1967).

3. "Stochastic Simulation and Forecasting Experiments with the Boughton-Brau Monetary Model," unpublished, 1969.

they were both generated by the same stochastic process can be refuted.
Preliminary results on this project support the validity of the model. Perhaps more importantly, these tests have shown that the use of deterministic
simulations, dropping the residual errors from each equation, introduces
very little bias into the simulation results.[1]

Figures 9 through 12 present the time paths for each of the four "target" variables in the model.[2] The solid lines trace the historical values,
while the dotted lines were generated by the model. The technique here
was to feed into the model the observed values of the exogenous variables
for each time period. For the initial period only, the observed values of
the lagged endogenous variables also were introduced; for subsequent
periods, the simulated values from the previous period were fed back into
the model. The equation residuals were not used. As mentioned above,
Geraci's results indicate that there is not likely to be any statistically
significant difference between the historical and simulated series for any
of these variables. However, a note of caution is in order. The presence
of autocorrelated residuals in several of the equations of the model shows
up clearly in the simulation paths, a fault which at least in theory could
undermine the descriptive and predictive capabilities of the model.[3]

The next step in validating the model is to attempt to predict movements in the target variables beyond the end of the estimation period (i.e.
beyond 1966). This test involves making ex post forecasts, so called because the values which the model is being called upon to predict are already known to us (but not to the model). The advantage of this technique
for validation is that it permits us to enter precise values of all

----

1. The possibility of such bias is discussed at length in E. Philip
Howrey and H.H. Kelejian, "Dynamic Econometric Models: Simulation versus
Analytical Solutions," The Design of Computer Simulation Experiments,
Thomas H. Naylor, (ed.) (Durham, N.C.: Duke University Press, 1969), pp.
207-231.

2. The computer program used for the simulations is described in
Appendix B.

3. E. Malinvaud, Statistical Methods of Econometrics (Chicago: Rand
McNally, 1966), pp. 420-472. On the other hand, Malinvaud observes that
the "bias...will be small if variability of the exogenous variables [in-
cluded in the regression] exceeds that of the errors and if the coefficient
a [i.e., the coefficient on the exogenous variables] is not near zero" (p.
464); and again "the bias in prediction will remain small in the models
now considered [i.e., first-order autoregressive models] if the evolution
of the exogenous variables during the prediction period follows the average
evolution during the estimation period" (p. 466).

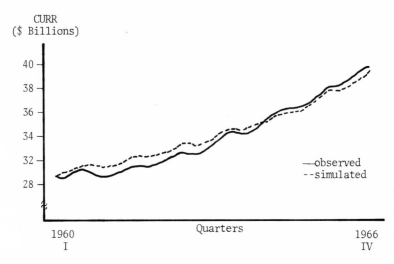

Figure 9.   Validation of the Monetary Model:
Simulated and Observed Values of CURR

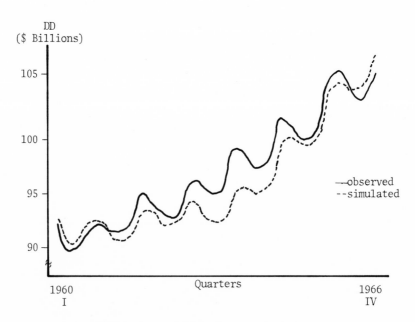

Figure 10.   Validation of the Monetary Model:
Simulated and Observed Values of DD

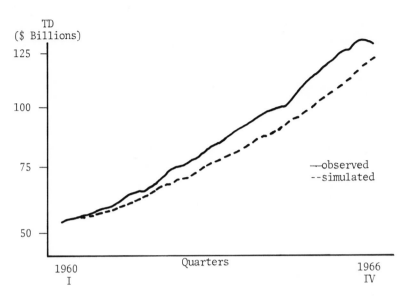

Figure 11. Validation of the Monetary Model:
Simulated and Observed Values of TD

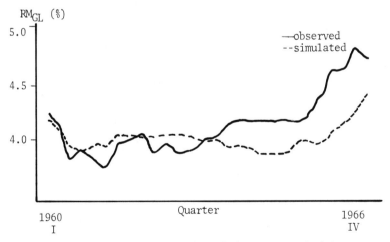

Figure 12. Validation of the Monetary Model:
Simulated and Observed Values of RM_{GL}

exogenous data, even for the period for which the forecasts are being made. There are two possible sources of forecast error: error in model specification and error in predicting exogenous data. An ex post forecast enables us to isolate the model from the latter form.[1]

The forecasts shown in Table 4 are preliminary results from the Geraci project and were made with an earlier but similar version of the model described above.[2] Predictions are made for each of the four quarters of 1967. For purposes of comparison, the forecasts of a "naive" model are shown; that model assumes that the change in 1967 would be equal to the change in 1966. Actually the comparison has been biased in favor of the naive model, since several different forms of naivete were tested and the one with the best results, ex post, was selected for presentation.[3]

The econometric forecasts are quite satisfactory for the two money supply aggregates but rather useless for the long-term bond rate. In the latter case the naive model performs much better, but still poorly. Although not shown, the individual components of the monetary targets, as well as most of the state variables, tracked pretty well throughout not only the four quarters of 1967 but also most of 1968. The model appears to be satisfactorily efficient in making predictions of quarterly movements for up to eight quarters in advance, if the exogenous variables are introduced accurately. On the other hand, no statistical tests of accuracy have been performed at this time. All that can be said is that the predictive record does not seem to provide evidence in refutation of the validity of the model specification.

Behavior of the Model under Exogenous Shocks

The next step in developing a test of the role of the funds market in transmitting policy changes is to determine the nature of the effects

---

1. Evans argues (pp. 516-517) that only ex ante forecasts comprise an "acid test" of a model, since good ex post forecasts always can be obtained through patient manipulation of the model. However, it would seem that if, as has been done here, the model is constructed without use of the data for the forecast period and is not respecified in order to improve the forecasts once they are obtained, the difference between the two types of test vanishes.

2. For a further discussion of forecasts with this model, see James M. Boughton, "Econometric Models: a Decision-Making Tool for Bank Management," Journal of Bank Research, I (Summer 1970), 9-19.

3. These naive models are described in Evans, pp. 516-518.

Table 4. Ex Post Econometric Forecasts of 1967 Values of the Monetary Targets

| | Target Variables | | | | | |
| | Money Supply ($ Billions) | | Broad Money Supply ($ Billions) | | Bond Rates (%) | |
Quarter	A^a	P^a	A	P	A	P
67 I	143.8	144.7	277.2	277.6	4.44	4.48
II	143.9	144.8	283.4	283.8	4.71	4.48
III	146.7	147.5	291.5	293.2	4.93	4.43
IV	152.0	151.4	299.6	301.3	5.33	4.72
Net changes 66IV-67IV	8.5	7.9	28.2	29.9	0.63	0.02
Naive model[b] forecast		(2.6)		(11.4)		(0.35)

a. A = actual observed value
   P = predicted value, generated by the model

b. Naive model: $\Delta Y_{67} = \Delta Y_{66}$.

Source: see text for complete description.

produced in the model when policies are changed. A set of computer simulations will be developed under different sets of exogenous data in order to generate local estimates of the model's policy multipliers. In the next section these multipliers will be manipulated so as to reveal the effects due to the funds market.

It should be emphasized at this point that for several reasons we shall not attempt to render precise quantitative interpretations to the multipliers computed in this section. First, because the monetary sector is being examined in isolation from the real sectors of the economy, the multipliers are unable to reflect the feedback which naturally occurs when monetary variables affect the real sector. For example, the effect of open market operations on the money supply is being measured in the absence of any induced change in investment spending or other components of aggregate demand.[1] Second, even if accurate multipliers were to be calculated, the increased accuracy would not be of any great value for the objectives of

---

1. This use of simulation of an isolated monetary sector is patterned after Frank DeLeeuw, "Financial Markets in Business Cycles: a Simulation Study," American Economic Review, LIV (May, 1964), 309-323. In that and in the present case, the limitation was necessitated by the absence of a consistently estimated real sector in the model.

this chapter. Certainly it would be an interesting project to evaluate the relative impacts of various policies and to discuss the absolute values of the financial system's static and dynamic multipliers;[1] however, our objectives here may be met with far more modest statistical resources.

In order to minimize the distortion produced by the omission of the real sector while still providing a dynamic setting for the analysis, the length of the simulation runs has been limited to ten quarters for the policy studies. The last ten quarters of the sample period (1964 III to 1966 IV) were selected, so as to maximize the quantitative importance of the Federal funds market in the system.[2]

Table 5 describes the control solutions to the model for each of the ten quarters. For the control run all exogenous variables including the policy instruments are entered at their observed historical values in each period. The observed values of the lagged endogenous variables are entered for the first quarter only, in order to start the system; then the model generates successive partial-equilibrium solutions.

The next three tables (6 through 8) describe the changes which are generated when one policy instrument is entered at a level different from the control value. In each case all exogenous conditions in the model are identical to the control run except for the stream of values for that one instrument variable. Each simulation is a vehicle for studying the effects of one variable in isolation. Three policy instruments have been selected for analysis:[3] unborrowed reserves plus currency, the open-market variable, is reduced by $500 million each quarter; the Federal Reserve discount rate is increased by one-half of a percentage point each quarter; and the ceiling rate on time deposits under Regulation Q also is raised by a half point.

---

1. See James M. Boughton and Thomas H. Naylor, "Independence of Monetary Policies: A Simulation Study," Applied Economics, II (1970), 121-132.

2. This effect follows from the very rapid growth in market participation during the period, compared with earlier years. The choice of ten periods as a horizon is, of course, arbitrary.

3. In preliminary work, all of the instruments in the model were examined. For many of them, the effects produced either were quite similar to those generated by one of the three included here (i.e., they were not really independent instruments), or else they were for various reasons either uninteresting or unacceptable. See James M. Boughton and Thomas H. Naylor, "Simulation Experiments with a Monetary Policy Model," in Thomas H. Naylor, Computer Simulation Experiments (New York: John Wiley and Sons, 1971), pp. 353-380.

Table 5.   Control Run: Simulated Vaues of All
Endogenous Variables with No Monetary Policy Changes

	64 III	64 IV	65 I	65 II	65 III	65 IV	66 I	66 II	66 III	66 IV
Targets										
CURR	33.58	34.22	33.96	34.34	34.94	35.69	35.47	35.83	36.44	37.07
DD	97.65	101.17	101.73	100.39	101.30	105.23	105.92	105.08	105.42	108.18
TD	100.72	103.55	107.65	111.13	114.36	117.81	122.33	126.77	130.87	133.68
RM_{GL}	4.06	4.07	4.05	4.12	4.14	4.09	4.19	4.25	4.35	4.52
State Variables										
CL	38.92	40.57	41.94	43.70	45.17	47.61	49.48	52.04	53.77	56.66
FF	1.08	1.26	1.62	1.44	1.40	1.81	2.16	2.18	2.14	1.94
RES_R	20.38	20.93	21.16	21.41	21.57	21.62	22.19	22.37	22.65	22.97
RES_F	0.34	0.35	0.68	0.24	0.18	0.69	0.84	0.70	0.51	0.07
RM_{CL}	4.90	4.96	5.00	5.05	5.08	5.16	5.34	5.45	5.59	5.86
RM_{FF}	3.32	3.52	3.52	3.92	4.00	3.75	4.02	4.22	4.47	4.95
RM_{GS}	3.29	3.55	3.52	3.77	3.77	3.72	3.91	3.95	4.16	4.79
RM_{TD}	3.43	3.58	3.61	3.65	3.69	3.73	3.99	4.04	4.10	4.17

Source: see Appendix B.

Table 6. Effects on Monetary Variables of a
Sustained $500 Million Decrease in RES_{NBC}

	64 III	64 IV	65 I	65 II	65 III	65 IV	66 I	66 II	66 III	66 IV
Targets										
CURR	0.01	0.02	0.04	0.07	0.10	0.14	0.19	0.24	0.31	0.38
DD	-0.37	-0.68	-0.94	-1.19	-1.43	-1.66	-1.88	-2.12	-2.36	-2.60
TD	-0.50	-0.93	-1.30	-1.65	-1.98	-2.31	-2.63	-2.97	-3.33	-3.79
RM_{GL}	0.09	0.07	0.06	0.05	0.05	0.04	0.04	0.04	0.03	0.03
State Variables										
CL	-0.10	-0.21	-0.35	-0.50	-0.69	-0.90	-1.13	-1.39	-1.67	-1.98
FF	-0.27	-0.29	-0.27	-0.25	-0.24	-0.23	-0.23	-0.23	-0.24	-0.25
RES_R	-0.08	-0.14	-0.20	-0.25	-0.30	-0.35	-0.40	-0.45	-0.51	-0.57
RES_F	-0.43	-0.38	-0.34	-0.31	-0.30	-0.29	-0.29	-0.29	-0.30	-0.31
RM_{CL}	0.07	0.07	0.07	0.07	0.07	0.07	0.06	0.05	0.04	0.03
RM_{FF}	0.38	0.32	0.29	0.27	0.25	0.24	0.24	0.24	0.24	0.25
RM_{GS}	0.35	0.29	0.25	0.23	0.22	0.21	0.20	0.21	0.21	0.22
RM_{TD}	0.00	0.00	0.00	0.00	0.00	0.00	0.00	-0.00	-0.00	-0.03

Source: see Appendix B.

Table 8. Effects on Monetary Variables of a
Sustained Half-Point Increase in RM_{TDM}

	64 III	64 IV	65 I	65 II	65 III	65 IV	66 I	66 II	66 III	66 IV
Targets										
CURR	0.00	0.00	0.01	0.02	0.02	0.03	0.05	0.06	0.08	0.10
DD	-0.07	-0.14	-0.21	-0.28	-0.35	-0.42	-0.49	-0.56	-0.64	-0.72
TD	0.28	0.56	0.83	1.11	1.38	1.64	1.90	2.15	2.39	2.53
RM_{GL}	-0.00	-0.00	-0.00	-0.00	-0.00	-0.00	-0.00	-0.00	-0.00	-0.00
State Variables										
CL	0.00	0.01	0.02	0.03	0.06	0.09	0.13	0.18	0.24	0.29
FF	-0.00	-0.00	-0.01	-0.01	-0.02	-0.03	-0.04	-0.05	-0.07	-0.09
RES_R	-0.00	-0.00	-0.00	-0.00	-0.00	-0.00	-0.00	-0.00	0.01	-0.01
RES_F	-0.00	-0.00	-0.01	-0.01	-0.02	-0.03	-0.04	-0.06	-0.08	-0.11
RM_{CL}	-0.00	-0.00	-0.01	-0.01	-0.01	-0.02	-0.02	-0.02	-0.02	-0.01
RM_{FF}	0.00	0.00	0.01	0.01	0.01	0.02	0.02	0.03	0.04	0.06
RM_{GS}	0.00	0.00	0.01	0.01	0.01	0.02	0.02	0.03	0.04	0.06
RM_{TD}	0.14	0.14	0.13	0.13	0.13	0.13	0.13	0.13	0.13	0.10

Source: see Appendix B.

Table 7. Effects on Monetary Variables of a
Sustained Half-Point Increase in RM_{FRB}

	64 III	64 IV	65 I	65 II	65 III	65 IV	66 I	66 II	66 III	66 IV
Targets										
CURR	0.01	0.02	0.05	0.08	0.11	0.16	0.21	0.27	0.33	0.41
DD	-0.42	-0.77	-1.07	-1.34	-1.58	-1.80	-2.00	-2.20	-2.38	-2.55
TD	-0.50	-0.94	-1.35	-1.73	-2.10	-2.47	-2.85	-3.23	-3.61	-4.08
RM_{GL}	0.09	0.07	0.06	0.05	0.04	0.03	0.03	0.03	0.02	0.02
State Variables										
CL	-0.24	-0.47	-0.68	-0.87	-1.04	-1.19	-1.33	-1.45	-1.57	-1.68
FF	0.23	0.31	0.35	0.38	0.39	0.39	0.39	0.37	0.35	0.33
RES_R	-0.09	-0.16	-0.22	-0.28	-0.33	-0.38	-0.43	-0.47	-0.52	-0.57
RES_F	0.08	0.14	0.18	0.20	0.22	0.22	0.22	0.21	0.19	0.17
RM_{CL}	0.17	0.13	0.09	0.06	0.02	-0.00	-0.03	-0.05	-0.06	-0.07
RM_{FF}	0.38	0.34	0.31	0.29	0.27	0.26	0.25	0.24	0.24	0.24
RM_{GS}	0.35	0.30	0.27	0.25	0.24	0.23	0.22	0.22	0.22	0.22
RM_{TD}	-0.00	-0.00	-0.00	-0.00	-0.00	-0.00	-0.01	-0.01	-0.01	-0.04

Source: see Appendix B.

It is necessary to examine each of these instruments separately in order to allow for the possibility that the effects of the funds market are different for different types of policies. The study of the instruments in isolation provides a complete test in the sense that the study of combinations of variables would add nothing to our knowledge; the model, though nonlinear in some variables, is linear in the instrument variables. The instruments enter independently of one another, so that the multipliers pertaining to any combination of policies may be obtained through the simple addition of individual multipliers.[1]

As was mentioned in the opening paragraphs of this section, the model as it stands permits only a qualitative study of the effects of policy changes. For this reason no effort will be made to compare multipliers among instruments. This type of comparison could be made, of course,[2] but it would add nothing to our understanding of the role of the funds market.

The effects of a reserve contraction on the target variables (shown in Table 6) are as expected and follow quite readily from the structural parameters of the model. Both demand and time deposits fall immediately and continue to do so. The increase in cash holdings is a spurious result, but the effect is quite small and does not affect the monetary multipliers very much. The effects produced on interest rates by the contraction are interesting. Short-term rates react, as expected, by rising sharply and by more than long-term rates. But even though the contraction is sustained over the ten quarters, the interest rates gradually begin to settle back to the control values. Interest rates respond to the rate of change rather than the level of reserves. While this concept may seem strange at first, it in fact is quite orthodox. The absolute magnitude of the money supply is relatively unimportant in a closed economy; it is only the change in the stock that temporarily generates interest rates higher or lower than their normal values.

As deposits contract in Table 6, so does the level of commercial loans. Free reserves fall immediately, absorbing most of the initial reserve contraction. It is the action of bankers attempting to restore desired holdings of free reserves that brings about the sustained contraction in loans

---

1. This linearity also implies that the policy multipliers will be independent of the magnitude of the exogenous shocks. For example, doubling of the size of the shock will produce twice as great an effect.

2. Fromm and Taubman, pp. 84-88.

and deposits. The result which is of the most importance for this study is
that the decline in free reserves also serves to dry up the supply of Federal funds. This is the sort of evidence for which we have been looking.
A priori, the effect could go either way, since banks are both demanders
and suppliers of funds. But in the quarterly model, it appears that
policy-induced declines in free reserve levels will have a strong enough
impact on the suppliers of funds to more than offset the stimulative effect
of increases in the prices offered for these funds. The decrease, moreover, is sustained throughout the ten-quarter horizon of the simulation
run. The question of what effect this decline has on the values of the
target variables will be discussed shortly.

If monetary policy is effected through discount rate changes rather
than through open market operations, a somewhat different picture emerges
(Table 7). Effects on the target variables are quite similar in the two
cases, as are the changes produced in most of the interest rates. Required
reserves fall in the same way. Free reserves, however, actually increase,
sustaining some growth in the volume of funds trading. Note that no effort
is being made here to compare the magnitudes of the policy changes. It is
entirely coincidental that a $500 million reserve contraction and a half-
point discount rate increase generate effects that are roughly similar in
magnitude. The coincidence merely facilitates comparison of the two data
streams.

The main difference in the pattern of effects caused by the two policy
actions is that changing the discount rate does not directly alter the size
of the reserve base and thus makes it easier for bankers to take remedial
action against deposit outflows by increasing, for example, the flow of
Federal Reserve funds. The implications of this difference will be examined below.

The third and final policy shock (Table 8), a change in the average
ceiling rate payable for time and savings deposits (RM_{TDM}), is interesting
primarily for the portfolio shifts induced by such action. Even though
demand deposits decline, time deposits expand by quite a bit more. The
asymmetry is made possible, of course, by the lower reserve requirements
applied to time deposits. Whenever the public shifts its assets from demand to time accounts, a series of secondary expansions and shifts may be
expected to follow. Therefore, if one accepts either a "broad money supply" or a "bank credit" variable as being an important monetary target,

then an increase in Regulation Q ceilings may be viewed as an expansionary
action.

Most of the variables in the model, aside from demand and time deposits,
are unaffected by the change. The average yield on time deposits rises,
as expected, but by less than the change in the maximum rate. Commercial
lending increases after a lag, reflecting a reaction to the increase in
total bank credit. After about five quarters, the system does begin to
tighten up: short-term rates rise to accommodate the increase in RM_{TD}
(although lending rates are roughly constant), so that free reserves and
hence Federal funds trading fall slightly by the end of the ten quarters.
On the whole, though, the only important effect is the portfolio shift.

Dynamic Impacts of the Federal Funds Market

The point was made earlier in this chapter (p. 121) that the impact of
a state variable upon another endogenous variable cannot be observed
directly, either in an analytical solution of the reduced form or in a
simulation study. The preceding section developed a preliminary analysis
of the effects of policy actions on the state variables of the Federal
funds market. In this section efforts will be directed toward gaining
information about the effects of those terms on the monetary targets. For
this purpose four different versions of the model will be employed. In
addition to Model I (the complete version described above), three versions
will be designed to eliminate particular effects of the funds market. Com-
parisons between these partial specifications and the full model can then
be made in order to find the effects which are invisible in the complete
version.

There are two ways to modify the model for the removal of particular
linkages, neither of which is completely satisfactory. The first involves
removing the linkage from the state variable (e.g., the interest rate on
Federal funds) to the target. The state variable is still treated as an
endogenous variable, but the model is respecified in such a way that this
variable has no impact on any other endogenous variables in the model. If
this reestimation can be accomplished without serious distortion of the
other parameter estimates, then the properties of the two models can be
compared to determine the nature of the removed linkages. On the other
hand, it must be recognized that this transformation represents a deliberate misspecification of the model; it may result in a serious distortion

of the estimated parameters.

A second method involves removing the linkage from the instrument variable to the state variable. In theory, this surgery should have the same effect as the first technique, except that it may produce different sorts of distortion. Under simulation, the model may be forced to adjust through "unnatural" channels, producing misleading results. The choice between these two methods must be made on an ad hoc basis, so as to minimize the resulting specification bias.

In order to examine the role of the funds market in the financial system it will be necessary to isolate the effects both of the interest rate on funds and of the volume of net transactions. The volume effects, as it happens, may be isolated quite readily and with very few problems. The only point at which FF affects the rest of the system is in the supply function for business loans. When funds trading increases, banks may be able to óffer a greater supply of loans at given prices; this in turn has an expansionary effect on deposits and the money supply. By removing this possibility from the model, we can determine whether its inclusion was making any significant contribution. Moreover, since the supply function is estimated with RM_{CL} rather than CL as the dependent variable, the change can be implemented without causing any great disturbance in the function. This results in the following relation being substituted for equation (36):

$$\Delta RM_{CL} = -1.00 - 0.11\ RM_{CL-1} + 0.14\ \Delta RM_{GS} \qquad\qquad (39)$$
$$\phantom{\Delta RM_{CL} = }(.32)\quad (.10) \qquad\qquad (.09)$$
$$+ 0.26\ \Delta RM_{FRB} + 7.66\ CL/(DD+TD)$$
$$(.14) \qquad\qquad (2.27)$$
$$\bar{R}^2 = .56$$
$$DW = 1.98$$
$$SE = 0.10 \qquad\qquad (1960\ I - 1966\ IV).$$

This version will be called Model II.

Isolating the effects of the funds rate is a more difficult task. RM_{FF} enters the model in three places: it is "determined" in equation (37), it affects FF in equation (38), and it affects the Treasury bill rate in equation (33). The simplest way to eliminate its impact from the model is to remove equation (37) and to treat RM_{FF} as exogenous. That method is used to construct Model III. It may prove to be a drastic alteration of the model's properties, since it implies that a change in the discount rate, for example, would bring no change in the funds rate, and the model would have to adjust in other ways. Therefore, a second method has been employed (Model IV): equation (33) is re-estimated so that changes in RM_{FF} do not affect the bill rate. A policy change will cause the funds rate to move, but these movements will be impotent. Some linkages are still present through equation (38), but, since FF is prevented from affecting the model, no harm is done.

The replacement of equation (33) used for Model IV is as follows:

$$\Delta RM_{GS} = \underset{(.09)}{0.04} - \underset{(.03)}{0.02} RM_{GS-1} + \underset{(.17)}{0.82} \Delta RM_{FRB} \tag{40}$$

$$- \underset{(11.22)}{34.87} \Delta (RES_F/RES_{NBC}) + \underset{(3.29)}{5.63} \Delta (BF_S/BF_{PUB})$$

$\bar{R}^2 = .60$

$DW = 1.73$

$SE = 0.24$ $\qquad\qquad$ (1951 I - 1966 IV).

The problems with this equation prove the wisdom of applying the other approach as well. The worst problem is that the discount rate absorbs most of the effect previously associated with the Federal funds rate. In addition, all of the parameter estimates become rather unstable.

In summary, four versions of the model have been described. Model I is a complete model of the sector and consists of equations (27) through (38). Model II is identical to it, except that equation (36) has been replaced with equation (39), so that the linkages between the volume of Federal funds trading and the monetary policy targets are removed. In Model III, the interest rate on Federal funds is considered to be exogenous; this version consists of equations (27) through (35), plus equations (38) and (39). The fourth model treats the endogenous determination of RM_{FF}, but the linkage between it and the targets is removed, along with the linkage from FF to the targets. That is, Model IV consists of twelve equations: 27-32, 34, 35, 37, 38, and 40. The differences between the multipliers generated by Models I and II can be associated with changes in trading volume, and Models III and IV enable us to analyze the effects of changes in interest rates.

Table 9 summarizes the dynamic properties of the four models through a comparison of their truncated dynamic multipliers. In general, a dynamic multiplier reveals the full response pattern of the model after an in-finite length of time is allowed, while a truncated dynamic multiplier

reduces the interval to a finite time span.[1] An additional wrinkle is
added here, in that the responses of each period are discounted to create
a present-value truncated multiplier.[2] The procedure used here is as follows. For each model, a set of ten-period simulations is run under each
of four different conditions; results are produced similar to those shown
in Tables 5 through 8. Then the changes generated by the policy shocks
over the ten-quarter horizon are compressed into scalars by computing their
present value. Each change is discounted by a constant interest rate, for
which purpose the value of the Treasury bill rate in the starting period
(3.43%) has been selected.[3] Next the present value of the sustained policy
shock is computed. The truncated dynamic multiplier is then defined as the
ratio of the present value of the change in the target variable to the present value of the change in the instrument variable.

Table 9. Truncated Dynamic Multipliers[a] under Four Versions of the Econometric Monetary Model

Instrument[b]	Model[c]	Target Variables		
		Money Supply	Broad Money Supply	Bond Rates
RES_{NBC}	I	2.09	5.26	-0.12
	II	1.96	5.06	-0.13
	III	0.57	1.48	-0.04
	IV	1.68	4.33	-0.11
RM_{FRB}	I	-2.25	-5.61	0.11
	II	-2.37	-5.79	0.11
	III	-1.15	-2.68	0.02
	IV	-2.44	-5.95	0.11
RM_{TDM}	I	-0.51	1.62	0.0
	II	-0.51	1.63	0.0
	III	-0.41	1.88	0.0
	IV	-0.51	1.62	0.0

a. Defined in text, above. A negative sign indicates that a de-
    crease in the instrument produces an increase in the target, and
    conversely.

b. For the nature of the policy actions employed, see p. 136.

c. Defined in text, pp. 143-145.

1. See Goldberger, pp. 78-83.

2. This technique is developed in Fromm and Taubman, pp. 98-101.

3. The selection of a rate is somewhat arbitrary but has little effect
on the results under the conditions prevailing in this model.

The crucial result from this exercise involves a comparison between Models I and II. The comparison can be made with a free conscience, because it constitutes a very direct test of the consequences of a Federal funds market which is used as a source of lendable funds. In Model I, every dollar of Federal funds sustains an additional dollar of commercial bank loans. In Model II, trading Federal funds merely redistributes reserve balances without affecting lending volume. The coefficients are forced to conform with the assumptions, but the other parameters of the model are quite stable under the transformation. Thus any difference between the multipliers of the two versions must be due almost exclusively to the action of volume changes on loan supply and hence on the monetary targets. If this action increases the size of a particular multiplier, then we will conclude that for that individual case the efficacy of monetary policy is increased. If the multiplier is smaller because of funds trading, then such trading may be said to be a partial offset to the policy action. It should be kept in mind that these multipliers are constructed for the exogenous values which prevailed over the period from the third quarter of 1964 through the end of 1966; they may not hold for other periods. Another caveat is that the estimation procedure has not enabled us to determine whether Model I or Model II is the better representation of reality. This difficulty will be dealt with after the multipliers have been examined.

Confirming the partial analysis permitted by the tabular results shown for Model I earlier (Tables 5 through 8), it now is quite clear that Federal funds trading enhances the effectiveness of open market policy or, at worst, fails to offset it. For both of the money supply targets, the multipliers of RES_{NBC} increase when funds trading is permitted to influence lending. As was shown earlier, this increase arises because the contraction in free reserves which results from the reserve outflow cuts off the supply of funds. In spite of the increase in the demand for funds (manifested in an increase in the rates being offered, as in Table 6), total trading actually declines, forcing still further cuts in the supply of bank loans. Both the conventional and the broadly defined money supplies fall more than they would otherwise.

It appears that the effectiveness of the reserve shrinkage in raising long-term interest rates is somewhat reduced by the volume activity; however, an examination of the period-by-period changes shows that the effect is the same for each model, except that in Model I the bond rate is one basis point lower than it is in Model II, starting in the eighth quarter of the simulation. This result probably is spurious. The differences in the monetary multipliers, on the other hand, are based on sustained differences in the simulated paths and are generated by well-defined linkages.

The discount-rate multipliers change in the opposite direction from the open-market policy effects. Because this type of action does not directly affect the supply of reserves and because it encourages other interest rates to change, the opportunities are ripe for offsetting the action through the funds market. As expected, the bond rate rises by about the same amount in both versions of the model, but the monetary multipliers are reduced when we permit the supply of funds to increase, enabling the banks to shift resources to the points where loan demand is highest.

The final group of multipliers reveal that the effects of Regulation Q are unaffected by the volume of funds trading, which is not surprising, since it already has been shown that those effects are almost entirely distributional in nature.

In spite of the highly tentative and cautious nature of the tests that have been made on the effect of changes in volume, it appears that some definitive conclusions may be drawn. We know on theoretical grounds that the partial derivative of the supply of bank loans with respect to the volume of Federal funds traded must be between zero and one. The empirical estimation of the model indicates that that coefficient may be nearer to zero than to one, although the inadequate data obscure that conclusion somewhat. If the coefficient is approximately zero, it is obvious that the efficacy of all types of monetary policies will be unaffected by changes in volume; recalling the observation of William Poole, the volume of trading becomes in that case a "relatively useless piece of information."[1] Moreover, simulation of the empirical model reveals that the relative elasticities in the system are such that a policy action which reduces the algebraic value of free reserves can be expected to force a reduction in the flow of Federal funds, reinforcing the effects being generated by the policy change. Therefore, regardless of the magnitude of the effect of this trading on bank loan supply, the system will be unable to bring off a successful offset. Policies such as changes in the discount

---

1. See above, p. 94.

rate may be offset to some degree, although this model at least indicates
that the offset is small relative to the total effect of the rate change.

The results obtained for interest-rate effects (Models III and IV) are
much less clear, but the general direction of those effects is unambiguous.
Whether policy is effected through open market operations, the discount
rate, or some other means, the banking system must change the Federal funds
rate contracyclically (i.e., in reinforcement of the policy action) in
order to attempt to create an opposing movement in total volume of lending.
Given a reserve contraction, for example, there is no doubt that the rate
will rise and that if this rise has any impact at all on the monetary sector, it will be to reinforce the restrictive effect of the contraction.
The only remaining question is whether, in cases in which the volume of
trading is tending to offset the policy action, the interest-rate action
will be sufficient to reverse this tendency.

Consider the RES_{NBC} multipliers under Models III and IV. The drastic
alterations to the model in construction of version III lead to the
apparent conclusion that nearly three-fourths of the effect of open-market
policy (i.e., three-fourths of the value of its multiplier) is induced
through changes in the interest rate on Federal funds. Far milder linkages
are revealed in Model IV, but the direction of causation is unchanged. The
true magnitudes probably lie somewhere between these two, judging from the
types of errors involved in estimating each model. Model III is bound to
overstate the importance of the interest rate in reinforcing monetary
policy, while Model IV is bound to understate that effect. Since the same
direction of movement is implied in either case, the sign of the true
derivative is unambiguous.

The discount rate multipliers, as before, yield more confusing information. Model IV implies a perverse reaction to policy; the interest
rate effects (comparing Models II and IV) actually reinforce the effects
on the targets. This perversity occurs only because of the changes in the
elasticities of the model under the respecification of equation (33). If
the parameters had been more stable, it is probable that the effect would
have had the opposite sign. Model III, as expected, indicates a very
strong offsetting effect. Finally, with the exception of the distortions
produced in Model III, it appears that RM_{FF} has no effect on the transmission of changes in RM_{TDM}, for reasons explained earlier.

Conclusions

The evidence cited in this chapter now can be summarized.

1. The positive relationship prevailing between the aggregate level of free reserves and the volume of net trading in Federal funds prevents the banking system from offsetting open market policy through attempts to increase the velocity of the reserve base. This conclusion is reinforced by the presence of some evidence that, even if the volume of trading were able to move against the current, it would have little or no effect on the values of the monetary targets.

2. Changes in trading volume, viewed in isolation, may constitute a partial offset to discount rate changes since that type of policy instrument does not have a direct effect on the supply of reserve funds. The question then arises as to whether the positive influence of interest rate changes will reverse the tendency; whether banks will have to offer such high rates to attract this greater flow of funds that a contractionary effect will be produced by that means. Here the evidence from the model is not conclusive. Different results are obtained under different specifications of the hypothesis.

3. Regulation Q policy is enacted largely through alterations in the distribution of assets in the public's portfolio. These alterations are not materially affected by activity in the Federal funds market.

Chapter Seven. Summary and Conclusions

The question with which we began--how does the Federal funds market relate to the transmission of monetary policy?--has been fragmented throughout this study into a large number of particulars. What is the nature of
the market? Who participates in it? Where do the funds come from and
where do they go? Does the market merely redistribute resources or does it
support new lending to the public? How does the market affect the demand
function for free reserves? Can idle cash balances be influenced enough in
the short run to alter the velocity of the reserve base? Does the market
prevent the Federal Reserve from applying appropriate policy actions? How
good a case has been made for each of the conflicting views on the market?
What role is played by the interest rate on Federal funds? How does that
rate relate to other interest rates and asset prices? Finally, a question
yet to be posed: where is the market going at the present time, and what
implications are there for the future conduct of monetary policy?

Answers to these questions have been given throughout the preceding
chapters with varying degrees of certainty. This concluding chapter is an
attempt to discover the relevance of those partial answers to the larger
question of the impact of the market on the enactment of policy decisions.
Some of the principal conclusions may be summarized as follows.

1. The Federal funds market is an important mechanism for the banking
system, not only as a means of short-run adjustment of reserve positions
but also as a continuing source or outlet of funds for many banks. The
short-run function led to its inception, but the market has matured during
recent years. Many small banks use the market as a regular secondary reserve or investment medium, taking advantage of its high liquidity and, for
such a liquid asset, attractive yields. Quite a few medium-sized and large
banks employ the market as a correspondent service, acquiring funds from
the small banks just described and selling funds in the money market centers. There, banks find the market to be a steady source of lendable funds.
Because these diverse functions are performed by the market, Federal funds

are a good substitute for Treasury bills, for other secondary reserve
assets such as commercial paper, for discount window credit, for interest-
elastic bank deposits such as negotiable time certificates, for Euro-dollar
borrowings, and for other types of short-term non-deposit liabilities.

2. The important growth periods for the market were the 1920's, the
early 1950's, and the middle 1960's. In each period the growth came primarily as a response to tight money, to contractionary effects of monetary
policy actions. During the Twenties the market flourished primarily in New
York City as an alternative to borrowing from the Federal Reserve for
short-run reserve adjustments. Thirty years later a national market evolved
in response to improvements in communication and in the stability of the
banking system. Then in late 1964 the money market banks decided to begin
to use the market as a continuing source of funds, by offering rates above
the Federal Reserve discount rate. During the Sixties thousands of banks
began using the market for the first time, because they found it to be
more convenient and flexible than alternative adjustment mechanisms. As
monetary policy became contractionary, alternative sources of funds tended
to become tighter and more expensive, and the Federal funds market became
relatively more attractive. Eventually, the restrictive effects reached
this market as well, and alternative sources again were used.

3. Today almost every large bank and a great many small banks, some
with only one or two million dollars in total deposits, participate in the
trading of Federal funds. The participation by the great mass of country
banks could be an important factor in enabling the market to be a source
of lendable funds, not only to individual banks but to the banking system.
To the extent that any bank has a demand for idle reserve balances that is
elastic with respect to changes in short-term interest rates, the system
will be able partially to offset the restrictive effects of monetary policy
by increasing the proportion of total reserves that actively support lending activity. Since most large banks hold virtually zero levels of idle
reserves, this effect must come from the activity of relatively small banks
if it is to arise at all.

4. Total purchases of Federal funds are concentrated in a very few
large money-market banks. One important consequence of the market, with
both economic and social implications, is that the market serves to funnel
liquid resources out of the countryside and into major cities. New York
City banks are the principal recipients of this flow.

5. The interest rate on Federal funds is one of the more important variables in the monetary sector of the economy. It is extremely sensitive to pressures on commercial bank reserve positions and therefore should be a useful barometer of the current (short-run) effect of monetary policy. It also is a good index of the true cost of borrowing funds for immediate credit. The Federal Reserve discount rate is a poor substitute for this purpose because of the hidden costs of borrowing from the discount window. Those hidden costs arise from the official view, expressed in Regulation A, that discount credit should be used only to cover very temporary imbalances and that continuous use of the window is inappropriate. The longer-term movements in the Federal funds rate also are useful. A cycle about five quarters long (peak-to-peak) between the funds rate and the Treasury bill rate reflects the pattern by which banks build up and run off their secondary reserve and borrowings portfolios in response to changes in monetary policy actions. The relation between the Federal funds rate and the Treasury bill rate is so important that a serious misspecification of the demand function for Treasury bills results when that relationship is omitted.

6. For trading volume to be a meaningful figure, one must assume that at least part of it represents the conversion of idle reserve balances into active funds. However, the record of the Sixties belies that relationship. The secular effect of the funds market probably has been to reduce the demand for free reserves, although it is difficult to isolate the individual determinants of the steady decline in idle reserves. The fact of that decline is unmistakable: excess reserves for all member banks now are about half of the levels which prevailed a decade ago, and they are continuing to decline. Under the 1968 revisions to Regulation D, permitting banks to carry over a 2% excess or deficiency to the following weekly reserve period, liquidity requirements have been still further reduced; on at least two occasions since the change was implemented, weekly average excess reserves for the system have been below zero.[1] Under these circumstances it would seem improbable that idle reserves could be reduced still further by interest rate increases. On the other hand, an easing of reserve policy could be met by rate reductions and accumulation of new idle balances, though the econometric results of Chapter VI do not reveal a

---

1. Excess reserves for the week ending October 23, 1968 averaged -$1 million. For the week ending September 23, 1970, average excess reserves were -$47 million. Source: Federal Reserve Bulletin.

significant effect of that sort.

7. The net impact of open market operations appears to be enhanced by the short-run action of the Federal funds market. The most effective reinforcement works through the interest rate on funds, but changes in the volume of trading also help. A contraction in the supply of reserves is felt immediately in a reduction in the level of free reserves. The interest rate then rises as bankers bid against one another for reserve balances. But the supply is not there under a general shortage of funds, so the total volume of trading declines. Other interest rates rise, and bank lending and deposits fall, reinforcing the effects operating through other markets in the sector.

The linkages prevailing under increased expansion of the reserve base (easing of policy) could not adequately be tested in the present study for two reasons. First, the econometric model is unable to capture the assymetry of policy effects; elasticities appear to be the same for tightening and for easing of policy, even though it is well known that contractionary effects are more binding on the system than are expansionary effects. Second, the data which were used for the empirical tests cover a period (1960 through 1966) when the tightening of policy dominated. There were periods of gradual easing early in the period, but the quite restrictive period climaxing in 1966 probably dominates the model's properties.[1]

8. The net impact of discount rate changes may be reduced slightly by short-run changes in Federal funds trading, but no clear pattern is revealed by the simulation study. A reinforcing effect is present, as the interest rate on funds may be expected to move in the same direction as the discount rate. However, trading volume surely will move against the desired effect, creating a minor offsetting action. The empirical results are unable to sort out the dominant effect.

9. Points seven and eight, viewed together, would seem to indicate clearly that short-run changes in the variables of the funds market, particularly in the interest rate, reinforce the effects of monetary policy actions. The secular effects are less clear. Even if one accepts the argument that the funds market has been a causal agent in the long-run

---

1. The moves toward a tight money market began in mid-1963 and gained strength through 1966. See William J. Frazer, Jr. and William P. Yohe, The Analytics and Institutions of Money and Banking (Princeton: Van Nostrand, 1966), pp. 607-614, for a concise summary of monetary policy actions over this period.

decline in excess reserve holdings, the implications of that decline are
somewhat ambiguous. The policy instruments of the Federal Reserve now are
more efficient because of the reduced slippage and because of the reinforcing effects of induced interest-rate changes. But if the central bank
is less willing to use those instruments out of a fear that it may destabilize the economy by using such powerful devices, the effectiveness
of monetary policy may be reduced. The discussion of this argument in
Chapter IV (pp. 86-88) led to the conclusion that it "seems to be the
work of a doomsday prophet." On the other hand, there is some recent evidence that the Federal Reserve is indeed unwilling to use the tools at its
disposal to control inflation. Witness the record of 1968, when the consumer price index rose by 4.7%: total reserves of member banks grew at a
6.6% annual rate, the money supply grew at a rate of 6.5%, and the broadly
defined money supply rose by 9.3%.[1] Perhaps, however, that was a special
case, in which the Federal Reserve officials were lulled into believing
that the surtax was going to do the job of controlling the economy;[2] monetary aggregates were far more stable during 1969, as tight policies were
rather vigorously applied. Another possible explanation is that fear of
upsetting the government security markets resulted in a failure to act in
1968, as it has before.[3] These forces, uncertainty about fiscal policy and
concern over Treasury financing, probably are far more important factors
than the Federal funds market could conceivably be in the observed immo-
bility of the Federal Reserve.

10. The Federal funds market has continued in recent years to provide
new lendable funds for large banks. There was very little overall growth
in the market from 1965 through 1968 when Euro-dollars and negotiable time
certificates of deposit were developing into glamorous liabilities. Those
markets have been forcibly stabilized since 1968 by Federal Reserve regulations.[4] More than twice as much money has been raised in the Federal funds

1. Federal Reserve Bank of St. Louis, "Monetary Trends" and "National
Economic Trends," May, 1969.

2. See Jerry L. Jordan and Charlotte E. Reubling, "Federal Open Market
Committee Decisions in 1968: a Year of Watchful Waiting," Federal Reserve
Bank of St. Louis Review, LI (May, 1969), 11-12.

3. Ibid., pp. 10-12. See also William P. Yohe and Louis C. Gasper,
"The 'Even Keel' Decisions of the Federal Open Market Committee," Financial
Analysts Journal, November-December, 1970.

4. In September, 1969 Regulation D was modified to include a marginal
reserve requirement on Euro-dollar liabilities. The growth of time

Table 10.   Selected Liabilities Held by Major Banks in the United States.

| | Amounts ($ Billions)[a] | | |
	End of 1965	End of 1968	End of 1970
Euro-dollars	1.3	7.0	7.7
Time Certificates	16.3	23.5	26.1
Federal Funds	1.5	3.4	8.3

a. The data for different instruments are not strictly comparable.
    Euro-dollars are defined as "liabilities of U.S. banks to their
    foreign branches." Time certificates include only those issued in
    denominations of $100,000 or more, by weekly reporting commercial
    banks. Federal funds are the net purchases of the net purchasing
    banks in the sample of 46 banks used by the Federal Reserve.

Source: Federal Reserve Bulletin.

market during the past two years (1969-1970) as in the other two markets
combined. Perhaps because it is the most harmless to the effectiveness of
monetary policy, the funds market may prove in the long run to be the most
stable and viable of those listed.

What has happened, then, to the very powerful argument presented by
Warren Smith and described in Chapter IV? His article clearly demonstrated
the possibility of velocity-increasing offsets to policy through a mechanism quite similar to the Federal funds market. He argued that it is the
"basic function" of the banking system to "mobilize the existing supply of
money more effectively...when credit conditions are tightened," offsetting
the contraction in the monetary base effected by the central bank. Furthermore, Hyman Minsky presented a cogent argument showing that this same
effect could operate through "institutional evolution," including the
growth of the funds market. However, the record of the past decade indicates that, while these effects do exist--the banks of the country do
attempt to mobilize financial resources as effectively as possible--the
relative elasticities in reserve and money markets simply do not permit
this effect to be strong enough to reduce the effectiveness of policy.

The one factor that is most important in stabilizing the role of the
funds market in the transmission of policy effects is the strength of the
Federal funds interest rate as an equilibrating force. The arguments of
the offset school rest on the inelasticity of credit demands to interest

---

certificates was controlled by a refusal to amend Regulation Q so as to permit time deposit yields to become competitive with open-market rates in 1969.

rate changes or on the inelasticity of interest rates to changes in the
supply of credit. In the empirical estimation of financial relationships
given in Chapter IV, both of these elasticities turn out to be large enough
to bring about the effects being induced by the central bank through their
policy actions, at least when those policies are effected directly through
open market operations.[1] The main reaction in the Federal funds market to
a reserve contraction will be an increase in interest rates without a significant increase in the volume of reserves being traded.

The interbank market for Federal Reserve funds is not a serious problem
and may be at least some help for the transmission of Federal Reserve
policy actions. It is an important aid to the commercial banking system
in conducting its daily operations. It therefore is both economically and
politically productive and has earned a continuing role in the functioning
of the financial sector of the United States economy.

---

1. The inference as to elasticities could be misleading; no attempt
has been made to estimate the elasticities of the model directly. See
Chapter VI (pp. 143-145), above, for a complete discussion of the techniques used.

APPENDIXES

Appendix A. Data Glossary

The data used to estimate the parameters of the empirical model are all seasonally unadjusted. The monetary variables are measured in billions of current dollars, and interest rates are in percentage form (e.g., a 4% rate is measured as 4.00). The variables are defined and explained below.

Target Variables

CURR   Currency liabilities of the Treasury and Federal Reserve banks, less currency holdings of commercial banks. That is, CURR measures the amount of currency held by the non-bank public. Source: Federal Reserve Bulletin.

DD   Demand deposits in member banks, net of cash items in process of collection and demand deposits due from domestic commercial banks; i.e., demand deposits subject to reserve requirements. Source: Board of Governors of the Federal Reserve System, "Aggregate Reserves and Member Bank Deposits," Release G.10 of the Division of Research and Statistics.

TD   Time and savings deposits in member banks. Source: same as DD.

RM_{GL} Market yield on U.S. Treasury securities maturing or callable in 10 years or more; used as an average rate on long-term government bonds. Source: Frank deLeeuw, unpublished data appendix to "A Model of Financial Behavior," (hereinafter referred to apologetically as "deLeeuw's appendix"); and the Federal Reserve Bulletin for the more recent quarters.

Note: as used in this work, CURR + DD serves as a proxy for the money supply, and TD is added to this sum to yield the broadly defined money supply; CURR may be subtracted to give the bank credit proxy as used by the Federal Reserve. The money supply data differ from the usual definitions in that non-member deposits are excluded. On the other hand, it is highly probable that the errors introduced by this omission are less than the errors removed, since the portion of total deposits being held in member banks has to be assumed to be constant in either case. This point is discussed further in Boughton, Brau, Naylor, and Yohe, p. 343.

State Variables

CL   Commercial and Industrial Loans made by weekly reporting commercial banks. Equations using this series have been estimated only for the 1960-66 period, since the data prior to that time are not quite consistent with the later period. There was another shift in the series during 1966, and the last two observations have been adjusted by the author to provide a consistent series. Source: Federal Reserve Bulletin.

Note: the ratio of CL to total member bank deposits is used extensively throughout the model. This could cause trouble if data shifts among classes of banks were extensive or erratic. While such shifts may occur in very short-run data, they have not been a problem in the series being used here. For the 28 observations used in the model, the ratio of deposits at weekly reporting banks to total member-bank deposits ranged from 0.61 to 0.63.

FF   Net purchases by the net purchasing banks in a sample of 46 major Reserve City banks. The choice of this measure is discussed at length in Chapter III. Source: Federal Reserve Bulletin.

RES_F Free reserves (nonborrowed excess reserves) of all member banks. When negative, this variable is often referred to in the literature as "net borrowed reserves." Source: same as DD.

RES_R Required reserves of all member banks, computed for a constant reserve requirement. Source: same as DD.

RM_{CL} Average interest rate charged by major banks for short-term business loans. Source: Federal Reserve Bulletin.

RM_{FF} Average rate paid by major banks for purchases of Federal funds. Source: Federal Reserve Bulletin.

RM_{GS} Market yield on 91-day Treasury bills. Source: deLeeuw's appendix and Federal Reserve Bulletin.

RM_{TD} Yield on time deposits at commercial banks. The basic series contains only annual data; the quarterly series used here was compiled from data estimated and reported in deLeeuw's appendix and in Hendershott, pp. 62-65.

Policy Instruments

BF_L Outstanding U.S. Treasury bonds; used as a measure of long-term government debt. Source: Federal Reserve Bulletin.

BF_{PUB} Total publicly-held marketable Treasury debt; used as the denominator for both long and short-term outstanding debt. Source: Federal Reserve Bulletin.

BF_S Outstanding Treasury Bills; a proxy for short-term debt. Source: Federal Reserve Bulletin.

DD_{GF} Demand deposits of the U.S. government placed in member banks; principally, these are held in Treasury Tax and Loan accounts. Source: same as DD.

RES$_{\text{NBC}}$ Unborrowed reserves plus currency; the principal Federal Open Market Committee variable. Currency is as defined for CURR; unborrowed reserves are the sum of free and required reserves, defined above.

RRR$_{\text{DD}}$ Reserve ratio required against demand deposits. This is an average ratio, weighted by the volume of demand deposits located at different classes of banks. The computations are outlined in Boughton, Brau, Naylor, and Yohe, p. 343.

RRR$_{\text{TD}}$ Reserve ratio required against time deposits. For most of the period considered by the model, there was only one effective classification in this context, so that the series could be obtained directly from the Federal Reserve Bulletin. Since September, 1966, multiple classifications have been used, requiring the independent computation of a weighted average requirement.

RM$_{\text{FRB}}$ Discount rate at the Federal Reserve Bank of New York. Source: Federal Reserve Bulletin.

RM$_{\text{TDM}}$ Maximum rate payable on time and savings deposits at member banks, under Regulation Q of the Board of Governors. A weighted average is computed from the ceilings which are applied to different classes of deposits.

Other Exogenous Data

C   Total personal consumption expenditure, durables and non-durables. Source: National Income and Product Accounts.

I   Business expenditures on new plant and equipment, plus net changes in inventories. Source: National Income and Product Accounts.

S   Personal saving; the algebraic difference between Y_D and C.

Y_D Disposable personal income. Source: Business Statistics.

W   Public wealth, computed as a weighted average of past values of GNP. The formula is

$$W = .114 \sum_{i=0}^{19} (0.9)^i \cdot GNP_{-i}.$$

The nature of this variable and its function in the model is discussed in Boughton, Brau, Naylor, and Yohe, p. 340.

Q_i, i=1,...,4   Quarterly dummies for seasonal adjustment. $Q_i=1$ in the ith quarter of each year, and $Q_i=0$ otherwise.

Δ First-difference operator:
$$\Delta X = X_t - X_{t-1} = X - X_{-1}.$$

Note: most of the data described above are quarterly averages of daily figures. The major exceptions are the time deposit yield, the derivation of which is explained above; the commercial loan rate, which is based on quarterly surveys; and the income components.

Appendix B. Computer Programs

The large quantities of data used in this study were processed with the aid of the IBM 360/75 operated by the Triangle Universities Computation Center and the IBM 360/30 operated by Duke University. The primary software employed for this work consists of the following FORTRAN programs.

1. Program ECON, a general regression program written at the University of Pennsylvania and adapted and revised for use with the IBM 360 by David Patterson and James Boughton. ECON contains options for several different estimation techniques; the one primarily used for this work was ordinary two-stage least squares. This program was used for the estimation of the model presented in Chapter VI and for the regressions used in Chapter I.

2. Program SIMULATE, a general simulation program written at the University of Wisconsin and adapted to the IBM system by Boughton, Patterson, and Miss Ellen Temple. For a nonlinear system such as the model used in Chapter VI, SIMULATE uses a set of iterative techniques to converge upon a solution to the model for each period of time. Of these, the present work used both the Gauss-Seidel and the Newton-Raphson techniques extensively. A complete description of the original Wisconsin version of the program and its solution techniques is given in Charles C. Holt and others, "Program Simulate II: a User's and Programmer's Manual," University of Wisconsin, Social Systems Research Institute, April, 1967.

3. Subroutine SPECTR, a spectral analysis routine written by Patterson and revised by Boughton, based on a program written at Princeton University by Herman F. Karreman. This program uses the Tukey-Hanning method for estimating the power spectrum. SPECTR was used to generate the spectrum shown in Figure 6 (p. 57). See Herman F. Karreman, "Computer Programs for Spectral Analysis of Economic Time Series," Princeton University, Econometric Research Program, Research Memorandum No. 59, July 15, 1963.

Bibliography and Index

Bibliography

Andersen, Leonall C. and Jerry L. Jordan. "Monetary and Fiscal Actions: A Test of Their Relative Importance in Economic Stabilization," Federal Reserve Bank of St. Louis Review, L (November, 1968), 11-24; and "Reply" to deLeeuw and Kalchbrenner, LI (April, 1969), 12-16.

_____ and Jules M. Levine. "A Test of Money Market Conditions as a Means of Short-Run Monetary Management," National Banking Review, IV (September, 1966), 41-51.

Anderson, Clay J. Evolution of the Role and Functioning of the Discount Mechanism. Washington: Board of Governors of the Federal Reserve System, 1966.

Baumol, William J. "The Transactions Demand for Cash: an Inventory-Theoretic Approach," Quarterly Journal of Economics, LXVI (November, 1952), 545-556.

Baxter, Nevins D. "Country Banks and the Federal Funds Market," Federal Reserve Bank of Philadelphia Business Review, April, 1966, 3-9.

_____. "Why Federal Funds?" Federal Reserve Bank of Philadelphia Business Review, August, 1966, 2-9.

Beckhart, Benjamin and James G. Smith. The New York Money Market: Sources and Movements of Funds. New York: Columbia University Press, 1932.

Board of Governors of the Federal Reserve System. Banking and Monetary Statistics. Washington, 1943.

_____ The Federal Funds Market: A Study by A Federal Reserve System Committee. Washington, 1959.

_____. The Federal Reserve System: Purposes and Functions. 5th Edition. Washington, 1963.

_____. Fifty-Third Annual Report. Washington, 1967.

_____. "Monetary Aggregates and Money Market Conditions in Open Market Policy," Federal Reserve Bulletin, LVII (February, 1971), 79-104.

_____. "New Series on Federal Funds," Federal Reserve Bulletin, L (August, 1964), 944-974.

_____. Reappraisal of the Federal Reserve Discount Mechanism: Report of a System Committee. Washington, 1968.

_____. Regulation A: Advances and Discounts by Member Banks. 12 CFR 201, revised effective February 15, 1955.

_____. Regulation D: Reserves of Member Banks. 12 CFR 204, amended effective September 12, 1968.

_____. Regulation Q: Payment of Interest on Deposits. 12 CFR 217, amended effective April 19, 1968.

_____. "Rulings of the Federal Reserve Board," Federal Reserve Bulletin, XIV (September, 1928), 656; XVI (February, 1930), 81.

Boughton, James M. "Discount Administration in Econometric Models," Southern Journal of Business, V (July, 1970).

_____. "Econometric Models: A Decision-Making Tool for Bank Management," Journal of Bank Research, I (Summer, 1970), 9-19.

_____. "The Effect of an Active Market in Federal Funds on the Transmission of Monetary Policy." Ph.D. dissertation, Duke University, 1969.

_____, Eduard H. Brau, Thomas H. Naylor, and William P. Yohe. "A Policy Model of the United States Monetary Sector," Southern Economic Journal, XXXV (April, 1969), 333-346.

_____ and Thomas H. Naylor. "Independence of Monetary Policies: A Simulation Study," Applied Economics, II (1970), 121-132.

_____ and Thomas H. Naylor. "Simulation Experiments with a Monetary Policy Model," in Thomas H. Naylor, Computer Simulation Experiments. New York: John Wiley and Sons, 1971.

Brainard, William C. and James Tobin. "Pitfalls in Financial Model Building," American Economic Review, LVIII (May, 1968), 99-122.

Brandt, Harry. "Reserves: Through the Window or From the Market," Federal Reserve Bank of Atlanta Monthly Review, XLI (September, 1956), 3-4.

_____ and Paul A. Crowe. "The Federal Funds Market in the Southeast," Federal Reserve Bank of Atlanta Monthly Review, LIII (January, 1968), 7-13.

_____ and Paul A. Crowe. "Trading in Federal Funds by Banks in the Southeast," Southern Journal of Business, III (April, 1968).

_____ and Robert R. Wyand, II. "Using a Sharper Pencil?" Federal Reserve Bank of Atlanta Monthly Review, L (November, 1965), 1-4.

Bratter, H. "Should a Federal Funds Transaction Be a Loan or a Sale?" Banking, LVIII (June, 1966), 37-38.

Brimmer, Andrew F. "Foreign Banking Institutions in the United States Money Market," Review of Economics and Statistics, XLIV (February, 1962), 76-81.

Brunner, Karl and Allan H. Meltzer. The Federal Reserve's Attachment to the Free Reserve Concept: A Staff Analysis. Subcommittee on Domestic Finance of the House Committee on Banking and Currency. 88th Cong., 2d sess., 1964.

_____ and Allan H. Meltzer. "Some Further Investigations of Demand and Supply Functions for Money," Journal of Finance, XIX (May, 1964), 240-283.

Cacy, J.A. "Tenth District Banks in the Federal Funds Market," Federal Reserve Bank of Kansas City Monthly Review, (November, 1969), 10-20.

Chambers, D. and A. Charnes. "Intertemporal Analysis and Optimization of Bank Portfolios," Analytical Methods in Banking, 67-86.

Christ, Carl F. "A Short-Run Aggregate-Demand Model of the Interdependence and Effects of Monetary and Fiscal Policies with Keynesian and Classical Interest Elasticities," American Economic Review, LVII (May, 1967), 434-443.

Clark, Lawrence E. Central Banking Under the Federal Reserve System. New York: MacMillan and Company, 1935.

Cohen, Kalman J. and Frederick S. Hammer. Analytical Methods in Banking. Homewood, Ill.: Richard D. Irwin, 1966.

Colby, William G., Jr. and Robert B. Platt. "Second District 'Country' Member Banks and the Federal Funds Market," Federal Reserve Bank of New York Monthly Review, XLVIII (May, 1966), 114-118.

Comptroller of the Currency. Studies in Banking Competition and the Banking Structure. Washington, 1966.

Crowe, Paul A. and Robert R. Wyand, II. "Using a Sharper Pencil? Part II," Federal Reserve Bank of Atlanta Monthly Review, L (December, 1965), 1-4.

Currie, Lauchlin. The Supply and Control of Money in the United States. Boston: Harvard College, 1934.

DeLeeuw, Frank. "Financial Markets in Business Cycles: A Simulation Study," American Economic Review, LIV (May, 1964), 309-323.

_____. "A Model of Financial Behavior," The Brookings Quarterly Econometric Model of the United States, 464-530. Edited by James S. Duesenberry and others. Chicago: Rand McNally, 1965.

_____ and Edward Gramlich. "The Channels of Monetary Policy," Federal Reserve Bulletin, LV (June, 1969), 472-491.

_____ and Edward Gramlich. "The Federal Reserve--MIT Econometric Model," Federal Reserve Bulletin, LIV (January, 1968), 11-40.

_____ and John Kalchbrenner. "Monetary and Fiscal Actions: A Test of Their Relative Importance in Economic Stabilization--Comment," Federal Reserve Bank of St. Louis Review, LI (April, 1969), 6-11.

Dill, Arnold. "Causes and Effects of Commercial Bank Innovation." Unpublished Ph.D. dissertation, Washington University, 1967.

Duprey, J.N. "Country Bank Participation in the Federal Funds Market," Federal Reserve Bank of Minneapolis Monthly Review, July, 1966, 3-8.

Eckert, James B. "The Federal Reserve 'Bank Credit Proxy'," Banking, LIX (May, 1967), 62-66.

Employment Act of 1946. Act of February 20, 1946, 60 Stat. 23; 15 USC 1021.

Evans, Michael K. Macroeconomic Activity. New York: Harper and Row, 1969.

_____ and Lawrence R. Klein. The Wharton Econometric Forecasting Model. 2d Edition. Philadelphia: University of Pennsylvania, 1968.

The Federal Reserve Act. Act of December 23, 1913, 38 Stat. 251; 12 USC 221, as amended effective September 21, 1967.

Federal Reserve Bank of Boston. "Bank Reserve Adjustments through Federal Funds," New England Business Review, August, 1961, 6-7.

Federal Reserve Bank of Chicago. "Deposits and 'Borrowed Funds'," Business Conditions, January, 1966, 5-11.

_____. "Money by the Day," Business Conditions, January, 1958, 11-16.

Federal Reserve Bank of Cleveland. "The Federal Funds Market Revisited," Economic Review, February, 1970, 3.

_____. "The Role of U.S. Government Demand Deposits in the Monetary Process," Economic Review, June, 1969, 2-11.

_____. "Trading in Bank Reserves," Economic Review, December, 1960, 2-8.

_____. "Trading in Federal Funds," Economic Review, October, 1961, 8-10.

Federal Reserve Bank of Kansas City. "Reserve Adjustments of City Banks," Monthly Review, February, 1958, 3-8.

Federal Reserve Bank of New York. "Federal Funds," Monthly Review, XXXII (March, 1950), 28-30.

_____. "Second District 'Country' Member Banks and the Federal Funds Market," Monthly Review, XLVIII (May, 1966), 114-118.

Federal Reserve Bank of Philadelphia. "How Banks Adjust Their Reserves," Business Review, June, 1952, 3-8.

Federal Reserve Bank of Richmond. "Federal Funds," Monthly Review, November, 1964, 8-10.

_____. "Federal Funds: A Unique Kind of Money," Monthly Review, May, 1958, 6-7.

_____. "Federal Funds in the Fifth District," Monthly Review, June, 1961, 8-9.

_____. "Federal Funds in the Fifth District," Monthly Review, September, 1966, 8-11.

Federal Reserve Bank of St. Louis. "The Federal Funds Market," Review, XLII (April, 1960), 2-5.

_____. "Monetary Trends" and "National Economic Trends," monthly statistical releases.

Federal Reserve Bank of San Francisco. "The Role of Twelfth District Banks in the Federal Funds Market," Monthly Review, June, 1961, 104-121.

Finney, Katherine. Interbank Deposits: the Purpose and Effects of Domestic Balances, 1934-54. New York: Columbia University Press, 1958.

Fox, Karl A., Jati K. Sengupta, and Erik Thorbecke. The Theory of Quantitative Economic Policy. Chicago: Rand McNally, 1966.

_____. and Erik Thorbecke. "Specification of Structures and Data Requirements in Economic Policy Models," Quantitative Planning of Economic Policy. Edited by Bert G. Hickman. Washington: Brookings, 1965, 43-86.

Frazer, William J., Jr. and William P. Yohe. The Analytics and Institutions of Money and Banking. Princeton: Van Nostrand, 1966.

Freeman, Louise. "The Financing of Government Securities Dealers," Federal Reserve Bank of New York Monthly Review, XLVI (June, 1964), 108-
116.

Fromm, Gary and Paul Taubman. Policy Simulations with an Econometric
Model. Washington: Brookings, 1968.

Gaines, Tilford C. Techniques of Treasury Debt Management. New York:
Columbia University and the Free Press, 1962.

Geraci, Vincent J. "Stochastic Simulation and Forecasting Experiments
with the Boughton-Brau Monetary Model," unpublished, 1969.

Gidge, Frederick. "Billion Dollar Specialty: Security Dealer Clearance,"
Burroughs Clearing House, XLVIII (August, 1964), 44-45+.

Goldberger, Arthur S. Impact Multipliers and Dynamic Properties of the
Klein-Goldberger Model. Amsterdam: North-Holland, 1959.

Goldfeld, Stephen M. Commercial Bank Behavior and Economic Activity.
Amsterdam: North-Holland, 1966.

_____ and Edward J. Kane. "The Determinants of Member-Bank
Borrowing: An Econometric Study," Journal of Finance, XXI (September,
1966), 499-514.

Gramley, Lyle E. and Samuel B. Chase, Jr. "Time Deposits in Monetary
Analysis," Federal Reserve Bulletin, LI (October, 1965), 1380-1404.

Granger, C.W.J. and M. Hatanaka. Spectral Analysis of Economic Time
Series. Princeton: Princeton University Press, 1964.

_____ and H.J.B. Rees. "Spectral Analysis of the Term Structure
of Interest Rates," Review of Economic Studies, XXXV (January, 1968),
67-76.

Griggs, William N. "Federal Funds Market in the Southwest," Federal Reserve Bank of Dallas Business Review, XLVI (November, 1961), 1-6.

Grossman, Herschel I. "A Stochastic Model of Commercial Bank Behavior,"
The American Economist, IX (Summer, 1965), 27-34.

Guttentag, Jack M. "The Strategy of Open Market Operations," Quarterly
Journal of Economics, LXXX (February, 1966), 1-30.

Hardy, Charles O. Credit Policies of the Federal Reserve System. Washington: Brookings, 1932.

Hendershott, Patric H. "Recent Development of the Financial Sector of
Econometric Models," Journal of Finance, XXIII (March, 1968), 41-65.

Henderson, James M. "Monetary Reserves and Credit Control," American
Economic Review, L (June, 1960), 348-369.

Hirsch, Albert A. "Adjusting Reserves Through the Federal Funds Market:
The Record of District Banks," Federal Reserve Bank of Atlanta Monthly
Review, XLVII (October, 1962), 1-3.

Hodgman, Donald R. Commercial Bank Loan and Investment Policy. Champaign:
University of Illinois Press, 1963.

Holland, Robert C. and George Garvy. The Redesigned Discount Mechanism and
the Money Market. Washington: Board of Governors, 1968.

Howrey, E. Philip and H.H. Kelejian. "Dynamic Econometric Models: Simulation Versus Analytical Solutions," The Design of Computer Simulation Experiments. Edited by Thomas H. Naylor. Durham, N.C.: Duke University Press, 1969.

Johnston, J. Econometric Methods. New York: McGraw-Hill, 1963.

Jones, David M. A Review of Recent Academic Literature on the Discount Mechanism. Washington: Board of Governors, 1968.

Jordan, Jerry L. and Charlotte E. Reubling. "Federal Open Market Committee Decisions in 1968: A Year of Watchful Waiting," Federal Reserve Bank of St. Louis Review, LI (May, 1969), 6-15.

Keran, Michael W. and Christopher T. Babb. "An Explanation of Federal Reserve Actions: 1933-1968," Federal Reserve Bank of St. Louis Review, LI (July, 1969), 7-20.

Keynes, John Maynard. The General Theory of Employment, Interest, and Money. London: Harcourt, Brace and Company, 1936.

——————————. A Treatise on Money. London: MacMillan & Company, 1930.

Klopstock, Fred H. "Euro-Dollars in the Liquidity and Reserve Management of United States Banks," Federal Reserve Bank of New York Monthly Review, L (July, 1968), 130-138.

Legislative Reference Section of the Library of Congress. "Independent Appraisal of Certain Rulings of the Comptroller of the Currency." Washington, 1965.

Lynn, Dolores P. Reserve Adjustments of the Eight Major New York City Banks During 1966. Washington: Board of Governors, 1968.

Malinvaud, E. Statistical Methods of Econometrics. Chicago: Rand McNally, 1966.

Martens, Edward J. Federal Funds: A Money Market Device. San Francisco: Pacific Coast Bankers School, 1958.

Mayer, Thomas. Monetary Policy in the United States. New York: Random House, 1968.

McKinney, George W., Jr. The Federal Reserve Discount Window: Administration in the Fifth District. New Brunswick, N.J.: Rutgers University Press, 1960.

Meek, Paul. Discount Policy and Open Market Operations. Washington: Board of Governors, 1968.

Meigs, A. James. Free Reserves and the Money Supply. Chicago: University of Chicago Press, 1962.

Meltzer, Allan H. and G. v.d. Linde. A Study of the Dealer Market for Federal Government Securities. Materials prepared for the Joint Economic Committee, U.S. Congress. 86th Cong., 2d sess., 1960.

Minsky, Hyman P. "Central Banking and Money Market Change," Quarterly Journal of Economics, LXXI (May, 1957), 188-205.

Monhollon, Jimmie R. "Bank Credit Proxy," Federal Reserve Bank of Richmond Monthly Review, March, 1970, 12-16.

_____. (ed.). Instruments of the Money Market. 2d Edition. Richmond: Federal Reserve Bank of Richmond, 1970.

Morrison, George R. Liquidity Preferences of Commercial Banks. Chicago: University of Chicago Press, 1966.

Nadler, Marcus and others. The Money Market and its Institutions. New York: Ronald Press, 1955.

Naylor, Thomas H. and J.M. Finger. "Verification of Computer Simulation Models," Management Science, XIV (October, 1967), B92-B101.

_____, William H. Wallace and W. Earl Sasser. "A Computer Simulation Model of the Textile Industry," Journal of the American Statistical Association, LXII (December, 1967).

_____, Kenneth Wertz and Thomas Wonnacott. "Spectral Analysis of Data Generated by Simulation Experiments with Econometric Models," Econometrica, XXXVII (April, 1969), 333-352.

Nerlove, M. and K.F. Wallis. "Use of the Durbin-Watson Statistic in Inappropriate Situations," Econometrica, XXXIV (January, 1966), 235-238.

Nichols, Dorothy M. "Marketing Money: How 'Smaller' Banks Buy and Sell Federal Funds," Federal Reserve Bank of Chicago Business Conditions, August, 1965, 8-12.

_____. Trading in Federal Funds. Washington: Board of Governors, 1965.

Ormsby, Priscilla. Summary of the Issues Raised at the Academic Seminar on Discounting. Washington: Board of Governors, 1966.

Orr, Daniel, and W.G. Mellon. "Stochastic Reserve Losses and Expansion of Bank Credit," American Economic Review, LI (September, 1961), 614-623.

Parry, Robert T., James L. Pierce and Thomas D. Thomson. "Progress Report on the Monthly Money Market Model," unpublished, 1968.

Patinkin, Don. Money, Interest, and Prices. 2d Edition. New York: Harper and Row, 1965.

Phaup, Marvin M. "Fourth District Trading in Federal Funds," Federal Reserve Bank of Cleveland Economic Commentary, (November 24, 1969).

_____. "Recent Developments in the Federal Funds Market in the Fourth District," Federal Reserve Bank of Cleveland Economic Commentary, (March 8, 1971).

Pierce, James L. "Commercial Bank Liquidity," Federal Reserve Bulletin, LII (August, 1966), 1093-1101.

Platt, Robert B. "The Interest Rate on Federal Funds: an Empirical Approach," Journal of Finance, XXV (June, 1970), 585-597.

Polakoff, Murray E. "Federal Reserve Discount Policy and Its Critics," Banking and Monetary Studies, 190-212. Edited by Deane Carson. Homewood, Ill.: Richard D. Irwin, 1963.

_____. "Reluctance Elasticity, Least Cost, and Member-Bank Borrowing: A Suggested Integration," Journal of Finance, XV (March, 1960), 1-18.

_____ and William L. Silber. "Reluctance and Member-Bank Borrowing: Additional Evidence," Journal of Finance, XXII (March, 1967), 88-92.

Poole, William R. "Commercial Bank Reserve Management in a Stochastic Model: Implications for Monetary Policy," Journal of Finance, XXIII (December, 1968), 769-791.

Prochnow, Herbert V. Federal Reserve System. New York: Harper, 1960.

Riefler, Winfield W. Money Rates and Money Markets in the United States. New York: Harper & Brothers, 1930.

Robbins, Sidney M. and Nester E. Terleckyj. Money Metropolis. Cambridge: Harvard University Press, 1960.

Robinson, Roland I. The Management of Bank Funds. 2d Edition. New York: McGraw-Hill, 1962.

Roosa, Robert V. Federal Reserve Operations in the Money and Government Securities Market. New York: Federal Reserve Bank of New York, 1956.

Rothwell, Jack C. "Federal Funds and the Profits Squeeze: A New Awareness at Country Banks," Federal Reserve Bank of Philadelphia Business Review, March, 1965, 3-11.

Sayers, R.S. Central Banking After Bagehot. Oxford: Clarendon Press, 1957.

Scott, Ira O. Government Securities Market. New York: McGraw-Hill, 1965.

_____. "The Regional Impact of Monetary Policy," Quarterly Journal of Economics, LXIX (May, 1955), 269-284.

Shearer, Ronald A. "The Expansion of Bank Credit: An Alternative Approach," Quarterly Journal of Economics, LXXVII (August, 1963), 485-502.

Smith, Warren L. Debt Management in the United States. Study Paper No. 19 for the Joint Economic Committee; Materials prepared in connection with the Study of Employment, Growth, and Price Levels, U.S. Congress. 86th Cong., 2d sess., 1960.

_____. "The Instruments of General Monetary Control," National Banking Review, I (September, 1963), 47-76.

_____. "On the Effectiveness of Monetary Policy," American Economic Review, XLVI (September, 1956), 588-606.

Stone, Robert W. "The Changing Structure of the Money Market," Federal Reserve Bank of New York Monthly Review, XLVII (February, 1965), 32-38.

Teigen, Ronald M. "An Aggregated Quarterly Model of the U.S. Monetary Sector, 1953-1964," Targets and Indicators of Monetary Policy. Edited by Karl Brunner. San Francisco: Chandler, 1969.

_____. "Demand and Supply Functions for Money in the United States: Some Structural Estimates," Econometrica, XXXII (October, 1964), 476-509.

_____. "The Demand for and Supply of Money," Readings in Money, National Income, and Stabilization Policy, 42-76. Edited by Warren L. Smith and Ronald M. Teigen. Homewood, Ill.: Richard D. Irwin, 1965.

Theil, Henri. "Linear Decision Rules for Macrodynamic Policy Problems," Quantitative Planning of Economic Policy, 18-42.

Tinbergen, Jan. On the Theory of Economic Policy. Amsterdam: North-Holland, 1952.

Tobin, James. "The Interest-Elasticity of Transactions Demand for Cash," Review of Economics and Statistics, XXXVIII (August, 1956), 241-247.

Toby, Jacob Allan. "Fed Funds," Federal Reserve Bank of San Francisco Monthly Review, September, 1966, 159-164.

Turner, Bernice C. The Federal Fund Market. New York: Prentice Hall, 1931.

Tyng, E. "Small Bank Problem: Utilizing Surplus Funds; Barriers to Activity in the Federal Funds Market and a Possible Solution," Burroughs Clearing House, XLV (February, 1961), 48-49.

U.S. Congress, Joint Economic Committee. Federal Reserve Discount Mechanism: Hearings. 90th Cong., 2d sess., September 11 and 17, 1968.

U.S. Senate, Committee on Banking and Currency. "Federal Reserve Questionnaires," Hearings before a Subcommittee of the Committee on Banking and Currency, (Pursuant to S. Res. 71), Appendix to Part Six. 71st Cong., 3d sess., 1931.

U.S. Treasury Department. Treasury--Federal Reserve Study of the Government Securities Market. Washington, 1960.

Watkins, Leonard L. Bankers' Balances. Chicago: A.W. Shaw, 1929.

Weight, G. Dale. "A Note on Some Sources of Nondeposit Bank Funds," Federal Reserve Bank of Cleveland Economic Commentary, (August 11, 1969).

Willis, Parker B. A Study of the Market for Federal Funds. Washington: Board of Governors, 1967.

_____. The Federal Funds Market: Its Origin and Development. 3d Edition. Boston: Federal Reserve Bank of Boston, 1968.

_____. The Federal Reserve Bank of San Francisco. New York: Columbia University Press, 1937.

Wilson, John S.G. Monetary Policy and the Development of Money Markets. London: George Allen & Unwin, 1966.

Woodworth, George W. The Money Market and Monetary Management. New York: Harper & Row, 1965.

Wyand, Robert R., II. "Money Market Conditions: What Are They?" Federal Reserve Bank of Atlanta Monthly Review, L (September, 1965), 1-4.

Yohe, William P. and Louis C. Gasper. "The 'Even Keel' Decisions of the Federal Open Market Committee," Financial Analyst's Journal, November-December, 1970.

Index

SUBJECTS